D0219476

JOURNALISM STUDIES

THE BASICS

'Martin Conboy's comprehensive introduction to Journalism Studies offers an invaluable guide to the history, future and central ideas of this significant, rapidly expanding and widely studied subject.'

Bob Franklin, Professor of Journalism Studies, Cardiff University

Journalism Studies: The Basics provides an introductory overview of the emerging field of Journalism Studies, discussing key issues and contemporary debates. Drawing on Conboy's extensive experience in the field, the changing nature of journalism and its future directions are addressed, through chapters covering:

- the history and development of Journalism Studies
- changing research methods and processes in journalism
- the impact of the 'end product' in wider society
- global perspectives on journalism
- technology and the future of the discipline.

Situated within a fast-growing and dynamic field of study, this engaging introduction will be valuable reading for students of journalism, media and communication, along with those seeking to develop a broader understanding of contemporary journalism.

Martin Conboy is Professor of Journalism History at the University of Sheffield. He has extensive experience of teaching and research within Journalism Studies in the UK and beyond. Widely published, he is the author of seven single-authored books on the history and language of journalism.

The Basics

JOURNALISM STUDIES

THE BASICS

Martin Conboy

LONDON AND NEW YORK

First published 2013
by Routledge
2 Park Square, Milton Park, Abingdon, Oxon OX14 4RN

Simultaneously published in the USA and Canada
by Routledge
711 Third Avenue, New York, NY 10017

Routledge is an imprint of the Taylor & Francis Group, an informa business

© 2013 Martin Conboy

The right of Martin Conboy to be identified as author of this work has been
asserted by him in accordance with sections 77 and 78 of the Copyright, Designs
and Patents Act 1988.

British Library Cataloguing in Publication Data
A catalogue record for this book is available from the British Library

Library of Congress Cataloging-in-Publication Data
Conboy, Martin.
Journalism studies / Martin Conboy.
p. cm. — (The basics)
Includes bibliographical references and index.
ISBN 978-0-415-58794-5 (pbk. : alk. paper) — ISBN 978-0-415-58793-8
(hardback : alk. paper) — ISBN 978-0-203-11385-1 (ebook : alk. paper)
1. Journalism—Study and teaching. I. Title.
PN4785.C63 2012
070.407—dc23
2011050421

ISBN: 978-0-415-58793-8 (hbk)
ISBN: 978-0-415-58794-5 (pbk)
ISBN: 978-0-203-11385-1 (ebk)

Typeset in Bembo
by Taylor & Francis Books

Printed and bound in Great Britain by the MPG Books Group

To my fellow travellers, especially Jane, Andy, Helen, Matthew and David.

INTRODUCTION

As I sit revising the draft of this book, the *Guardian* newspaper reports that Lord Patten, the chairman of the BBC Trust, has expressed concerns that the BBC, despite its role as a public service broadcaster, is inhibited in pursuing certain lines of enquiry such as those opened up by the hacking scandal at the *News of the World* for fear that it could be accused of political bias. This is a very worrying inability in Britain's most important journalism institution. This admission was included in a speech to the Society of Editors' annual conference on the eve of the opening of the Leveson Inquiry into the issues emerging from the phone hacking scandal. Both Patten's intervention and the inquiry itself are striking examples of how discussion of the practices of journalism in contemporary Britain remains of vital political and social importance. Studying journalism has never been more important as public and politicians begin the reassessment of what journalism is for and how it should be conducted. Put simply, Journalism Studies is part of that fascinating ongoing debate.

HOW THE BOOK FITS INTO THE SERIES

The aim of this series of books is to provide a clear and carefully structured introduction to a particular field of knowledge. This book will introduce you to Journalism Studies. Although this name will be used throughout the book, it is fair to alert readers from the start that some courses which teach journalism, and some research and commercial publications, will use the name "Journalism" while others will consider it as part of Media Studies. "Journalism Studies" will be used as an overarching term to encompass all critical engagement with journalism, however it is badged. Entitling the book *Journalism Studies: The Basics* is also a declaration of intent. It signals that in the view of this author the subject has generated enough critical and intellectual capacity to be considered as distinct from Media Studies and as something more reflective than implied by the word "Journalism" used in isolation.

The book is aimed at beginners with no previous experience of the subject and therefore the structure is intended to act as a guide to the main aspects of Journalism Studies. As far as the intended audience is imagined, the book may well be the first step in considering whether to study this subject at university. It may also satisfy the curiosity of a quizzical general reader or provide context to a journalist, perhaps surprised that his/her daily routines are drawing such levels of analytical inspection. The style of the book is intended to provide as accessible an introduction as possible, not simply to provide information but to make the subject interesting and engaging. I hope that it will enable interested readers to develop further their understanding within a carefully considered framework.

WHAT THIS BOOK WILL DO

Although an introduction, this is not an introductory guide to journalism as such. It will not explain how to do journalism or how to get a job in journalism, although it will explore the channels for education and training which have opened up as the subject of Journalism Studies has expanded at university level in Britain. It will also consider how these courses fit within the traditional routes into journalism. In fact, going beyond a description of this process, the book will outline discussions on what has become one of the fastest-growing areas of study within the higher education sector and it will also indicate the ways in which professional journalists have responded to this renewed scrutiny of their work.

The book is meant as a springboard into the discussions which have accompanied journalism over the past twenty years, during which time it has seen academic approaches to its study become established in university circles. Despite the relative novelty of Journalism Studies as a named area of academic study, the book will also be careful to relate its growth to longer traditions within the social sciences, historical approaches and also to the broader social and political debates which have accompanied journalism across the centuries.

HOW THIS BOOK IS STRUCTURED

The book is divided into seven chapters. **Chapter One** sets the scene and introduces definitions of both journalism and Journalism Studies. **Chapter Two** cuts straight to debates about how journalists have been prepared for their work and how this has changed as expectations of graduate-level education have become the norm for entry into journalism. **Chapter Three** considers the ways in which Journalism Studies has borrowed from other disciplinary areas to lay claim to establishing its own mix of approaches to research. **Chapters Four** and **Five** follow on from the traditions of research within which Journalism Studies fits. They concentrate on empirical and substantive discussion of the processes and the products of journalism, including alternative approaches to journalism outside the commercial mainstream. At all times I will highlight how such research acts to critique current practices and products in ways which seek to establish exactly what it is that journalism contributes to the contemporary world. **Chapter Six** looks beyond the parochial to consider international perspectives on journalism, from the imperial to the global. **Chapter Seven**, the final chapter, of necessity the most contemporary in its relevance, deals with journalism's engagement with technology. It stresses that this is nothing new but merely the most recent example of a particular communication form being forced to negotiate the introduction of new technologies into its traditional forms of practice.

HOW TO USE THE BOOK

The book is intended as an introduction. It may be read at face value or it may be used to develop further knowledge about its subject matter. You need not read it cover to cover as it is written and there is therefore some necessary contextual overlap between some of the chapters to enable it to be dipped into from any starting point.

A key aspect of the book's ambition to foster wider consideration of its subject matter lies in its Further Reading sections. Debates within the book necessarily provide only a sample of the wealth of discussion in the field of Journalism Studies. These sections at the end of each chapter provide guidance in a carefully selected range of reading which will enhance understanding of particular topics and allow readers to continue developing their knowledge beyond the basics in a logical progression, depending on their interest. They represent the tip of an iceberg of reading on what has become a very rich area and one which this book argues merits attention on account of the complexity and very real importance of journalism's contribution to our society. The lists are contextualized and annotated so that there are explanations why particular texts are of interest. While the focus in the Further Reading sections is on the contemporary, wherever possible they will include work which embraces the historical context of Journalism Studies as well.

STUDIES OF JOURNALISM
THE BEGINNINGS

INTRODUCTION

The systematic exploration within a university environment of the history, practices and processes of journalism and their political and cultural impacts has never been without its critics. Let's start our exposition by considering the following statement by a senior journalist who has direct experience both of working at a leading university and of publishing both by himself and in co-operation with professional academics on the subject of journalism:

> Professional journalists, especially British ones, are given to disdain for the work of media scholars ... but ... journalists would do a better job for the citizens they presume to serve if they encouraged more critical interrogation of the way journalism works.
>
> (Hargreaves, 2005)

This book will explore the development in Britain of an area of academic study which has emerged quite recently: Journalism Studies. The subject of this introductory text is, institutionally, the name often given to the study of journalism within a critical and often academic setting. It is located almost exclusively within the university sector, although this book will stress the often essential contributions made by journalists from outside this arena. It will look at the sorts of critical interrogation which both scholars and journalists who are interested in the civic and cultural impact of journalism have brought to contemporary considerations of its practice. On the one hand, such study could be considered as having had a long gestation period; on the other hand, it could be considered as constituting, especially in Britain, a short yet dynamic moment in the longer history of communication studies.

WHAT IS THERE TO STUDY?

So how can we begin to define our subject? What is journalism? Within a wide geographical, historical and generic range it seems to be definable by two aspects: its aim is to provide a truthful account of the contemporary world; and it is committed to reporting information that is new about that world, whether in terms of fact or opinion based in fact. This initial definition can be refined. Beyond these assertions, it is, in addition, a variety of technologically mediated communication, a traditional contribution to our democratic culture and a form of entertainment or commentary. Analytically, journalism tends to shape specialist knowledge for a non-specialist readership. On account of this characteristic, in order to produce journalism we need people who can digest complex information and prepare it for general consumption. Journalism explores, for instance, the decisions of politicians and other socially important groups and measures them against socially shared frameworks of ethical and legal behaviour. Furthermore, it is published on a regular basis and in a consistent format with a title and an editorial identity which most often includes a stable political worldview. In addition, it is directed towards a geographically dispersed and anonymous community. It achieves all this while articulating its audience within a clearly defined idiom, meaning that it is accepted as authentic by its audience because it speaks the same language. Given all that journalism aims to achieve, you can see that there is a lot to study!

JOURNALISM AS ENGAGEMENT WITH AUDIENCE

As we have defined it above, journalism is nothing new. The careful construction of an audience for discussions of topical matters can be seen in the periodicals of the early eighteenth century such as *the Tatler* and *the Spectator* as they sought to express the tastes and opinions of the rising bourgeois classes. Two hundred years later, in the very different media of first radio and then television, the BBC fashioned a national audience through its news bulletins and, in the popular press, from Rupert Murdoch's purchase of the paper in 1969, the *Sun* has provided a hugely successful and profitable articulation of a blue-collar, anti-authoritarian conservative populism for its community of readers.

Journalism is, in all its aspects, a type of communication which invites, at least in theory, the public into discussion. This is not just a modern consideration pandering to the possibilities of electronic communication of texts and e-mail but a traditional characteristic of journalism which goes all the way back to its beginnings. At one point in journalism's evolution, this communication with readers as contributors was a literal transaction. Periodicals were so restricted by political pressure in their provision of news and commentary that any controversial contributions came from the pens of the letter-writers, and in fact these often provided the main fare. A notable political commentator wrote under the alias of 'Cato' on the *London Journal* in the early eighteenth century. His provocative criticism of the South Sea Bubble investment disaster – a ruinously speculative financial venture with remarkably modern parallels with the 2008 sub-prime mortgage crisis and the economic disaster it triggered – was demonstration enough of the need for direct government intervention. Prime Minister Walpole bought the paper and replaced its staff in order to ensure the restriction of its political authority. Later in the century, a second notorious and anonymous letter writer was 'Junius', who boosted the sales and therefore also the standing of the *Public Advertiser* with withering commentary on the King's conduct of politics, including one particularly famous contribution on 19 December 1769 when he observed:

> Sire – it is the misfortune of your life ... that you should never have been acquainted with the language of truth, until you heard it in the complaints of your people. It is not, however, too late to correct the error.

Such letters had the effect of boosting the circulation of a publication whose other content was a rather dull digest of commercial information, official court announcements and, as the title of the publication implies, the extremely profitable complement to journalism: advertising. The necessity for the public to be invited into the discussions of journalism has remained and is today extraordinarily prominent not only in letters and phone calls but in e-mails, texts, blogs and tweets on the topics and personalities of the moment.

WHO ARE THOSE DOING THE STUDYING?

Journalism Studies is chiefly the work of academics and critics from a range of disciplinary backgrounds, including off-duty journalists, in dialogue with the work of students at both undergraduate and postgraduate levels. Together they make the case why, in the words of American journalism professor Barbie Zelizer, we need to take journalism seriously. It has been in evidence in our universities for a little over fifteen years under its present name and has come to combine both academic critique and research, together with thoughtful interventions from practitioners, some of whom are now working themselves as educators and researchers within the academy. It is this, often imperfect but still stimulating, exchange of views from commentators, consumers and producers which makes the field as vibrant and full of potential as it is today.

Academic research into journalism and even an appreciation of journalism as a range of communicative styles and genres has lagged behind the historical development of its subject, certainly in comparison to other fields of professional practice. This is almost certainly on account of the disdain of elite culture for much of journalism's output, a suspicion that this 'fugitive literature' – tomorrow's cat-tray liner – is at best a form of sub-literary output and at worst a form of communication ultimately corrupted by its overriding need to turn a profit. The figure of the desperate and unscrupulous journalist who will sell his children's toys for a decent story and who knows no bottom to the barrel in his pursuit of the squalid and the sensational is a familiar character in the popular imagination and has been represented in various guises in book, film and television programme over the years. In fact, as I write this book, this squalid tradition of journalism is taking on a new and very shocking sense of reality; no need for fictional accounts of grubby and illegal practices in July 2011, when the reality of the hacking into the mobile phone of the murdered teenager Millie Dowler by the *News of the World* was all too prominent in the world's news media!

A DECLINING REPUTATION

Such negative assessments of journalism are nothing new. They were already much in evidence in the early nineteenth century even as it began to establish itself as a political and economic force. Newspapers began to flourish commercially following the lifting of taxes on them after 1855, yet social, political and cultural elites tended to disapprove of the very tendencies towards popularization which made them so enormously profitable. The success of daily journalism from this point marks a separation between journalism and literature. Before this period, many contributors to journals and periodicals had also spanned a dual existence as writers who aimed at posterity in their creative endeavours, whereas popular journalism required professional journalists whose aim was to fulfil the demands of readers very much rooted in the present. The stuff of this new commercially successful journalism as well as its practitioners tended to be looked down upon, as they were considered to be producing a form of writing which was designed for the moment, an ephemeral product as opposed to the serious writing which traditionally aspired to lasting influence in Victorian Britain, beyond the concerns and tastes of the everyday and aspiring to the immortal uplands of classic status. Serious writing was considered to need investment in time and effort, a reservoir of artistic talent, and was presumed therefore to be a slow business. Journalism, by comparison, appeared to suffer through being composed in haste. The increasing commercial drive to sensationalization which accompanied the success of journalism over the century did not help and the corresponding genre of melodrama so prevalent within journalism was perceived by elite cultural critics as cheap, formulaic and only of interest to the lower classes. Debates on the nature and values of journalism echoed through the century, as the argument centred on whether the press influenced the people or whether the reverse was true and the press was, as it often claimed itself, genuinely reflecting the views of its readers. Journalists themselves, particularly of the everyday kind, had little inclination and still less time to add to these discussions and the debate was led, by and large, by elite commentators with their own political perspectives, not to mention prejudices, to pursue. So journalism arrived in the twentieth century with a great deal of negative cultural baggage, despite being a hugely profitable and influential communication form.

WHY STUDY JOURNALISM?

If Journalism Studies is, put simply, the study of journalism (as opposed to its transient consumption), then we might stop to ponder why we should study it at all rather than treat is as it is apparently intended: consume and move on! To a large extent, the role of this book is to explore why it is worth investing effort in studying a product intended for the moment. In short, we can answer that journalism draws upon and contributes to social and political realities. It goes a long way to creating our shared understanding of the world and of the place of our communities in that world. Surely, therefore, it is important to study these contributions. Even though it may be designed for consideration in the present, studying the longer-term impact of journalism enhances debate on why journalism matters in contemporary society and how we can enable it to preserve its best social impulses into the future.

THE DEVELOPMENT OF JOURNALISM STUDIES: THE BRIEF ACCOUNT!

This chapter will briefly assess the development of studies of journalism from the frenzied discussions of the mid-Victorian period to the foundation of the first schools of journalism in the late nineteenth and early twentieth centuries and to the steady reinvigoration of these studies through the twentieth century to the present day.

Journalism Studies is a new coinage for something which has been going on for some considerable time. Indeed journalism has been studied for a lot longer than it has been called journalism. Two dates frame that observation: 1690 and 1833. In 1690, a young

German scholar, Tobias Peucer presented a doctoral dissertation which is believed to be the first formal and extended study of news and news reporting, processes and practices: *De relationibus novellis* (Atwood, 2001).What he had studied was variously referred to in English at that time as Newes, Information, Advices, Observations, Tydings, Passages, Relations, Posts and Accounts, and these were produced by authors referred to variously as curranters, mercurists, newsmen, newsmongers, gazetteers, diurnalists and eventually journalists. The second date is the moment when the word 'journalism' first entered the English language from the French in an article in the *Westminster Review* in 1833. Its arrival in the language is considered to be exactly the moment at which a new word became necessary in order to capture the particular range of the periodical publications which encompassed both discussion of high politics side by side with accounts of crime and scandal from the police courts.

The import of 'journalism' into the English language is a convenient moment to begin a consideration of how journalism began to be studied: first, informally, and, later, with an increasingly formal critical edge. At the point when the word was coined, we are beginning to see the division between styles of writers. Some were primarily political pamphleteers – often with literary ambitions – such as English radical pamphleteer William Cobbett (1763–1835), the essayist William Hazlitt (1778–1830) and the revolutionary scribe whose work paved the way for both the American and French revolutions, Thomas Paine (1737–1809). In contrast to these, there were others of a more commercial bent who were content to target specifically commercial audiences with their writing. This tendency became consolidated once the taxes on newspapers, which had hitherto restricted circulation growth, were lifted from 1855, and a free market in journalism was inaugurated in Britain.

Discussion of journalism was rife in the quarterly periodicals, the prestigious publications of the Victorian era. There may not have been the institutional framework of the university to provide a sustained level of enquiry into the popularity and influence of journalism at this time, but these critical quarterlies and, later in the century, the monthlies, nevertheless provided a great deal of commentary and opinion on the subject. One of the most famous and influential analyses of journalism came in one such journal, the *Nineteenth Century*, in 1887. It dealt with the introduction of a range of stylistic features, largely imported from the better developed commercial environment for journalism in the United States. This style was named the 'new journalism' by cultural critic Matthew Arnold, who claimed that despite its evident energy it suffered from one irredeemable fault: it was 'feather-brained'. Despite such elitist disdain, journalism proved enormously profitable, the more so, it seemed, as it embraced a mass market which was willing to consume it. As a consequence the characteristics of popular journalism were disseminated throughout newspapers and were continually refined in their impact on culture in general.

Until this point, studies of journalism had been, by and large, restricted to occasional outbursts of prejudice, often informed by a fear of an increase in the influence of the poor, who had been further encouraged to read through the introduction of compulsory and free primary education from 1870. The journalists themselves generally kept out of discussions of journalism and its cultural impact unless, in the case of senior members of the industry, they turned their hands to writing celebratory accounts of their own working lives. This meant that the range of opinion on journalism seemed to be restricted to a span between elite cultural revulsion and self-regarding autobiography. This is not to say that more established academic disciplines had not already begun to consider journalism as a subject worthy of attention. Historians in particular had begun to produce the first of a number of Victorian accounts of English journalism. Alexander Andrews's *The History of British Journalism*, which appeared in 1859, and Bourne's *English Newspapers*, in 1887, provided something of the grand narrative of which the Victorians in particular were fond, as well as the template for many contemporary accounts within academe and among journalists themselves reflecting on the history of their 'trade'.

By the beginning of the twentieth century, the general elite response to any analysis of journalism ranged from suspicions of the motives of the press barons of the early twentieth century to the anxieties of influential commentators such as Queenie Leavis, the wife of famous English literary scholar F.R. Leavis, concerning what she perceived as the damaging moral effects of the popular press. This continued up until the 1930s, when an American stream of applied social investigation prised open the door to a more fruitful engagement. Although this is, by design, a largely British-based account of the development of Journalism Studies, the impact of American practices on the content of journalism as well as upon its study, including how journalists are educated, has been significant and is worth considering here.

THE AMERICANS TAKE CHARGE

In confirming the centrality of journalism to civic and cultural life, one of the most prescient debates of twentieth-century democracy concerned the role of the journalist. Walter Lippman, an American intellectual, reporter and political commentator, had in 1922 formed a very public view that society had become too complex for journalism to represent effectively and, in order to rectify this imbalance, he proposed that a cadre of professional political com-municators should be entrusted to disseminate a digest of what could be understood by the broader public. John Dewey, his intellectual antithesis, a philosopher and educational reformer, dis-agreed and argued instead for a better educated citizenry and for the central role of journalists in assisting in the extension of public interest in public affairs. Such discussion heralded a more considered approach to journalism as a social product which depended on the reader as a politically engaged subject as much as on the investigative and explanatory work of the journalists themselves. The publications most associated with this pioneering approach came from the Chicago School of Sociology, where Dewey was joined by George Herbert Mead and Robert Park. Park is the author of 'The Natural History of the Newspaper' (1924), an exploration of the place of communication in symbolic constructions of urban space, in other words how newspapers help us understand the cities we inhabit. This proved hugely influential in foregrounding the com-bination of social conditions and institutional structure which gave rise to the journalism of a particular age. Despite its indisputable impact, it had been preceded in Britain by Angell's (1923) *The Press and the Organisation of Society*, which was written from an explicitly socialist perspective. This indicates that well-considered social and political critiques of journalism were well under way across the English-speaking world by the first quarter of the twentieth century.

There had been a great deal of anxiety in the 1930s about the effects of mass media on susceptible populations which found expression in early considerations of the power of the media via the Frankfurt School. These scholars, most notably Adorno and Horkheimer, had a significant effect on the early literature of Media Studies and then Journalism Studies. They had observed at first hand the rise of fascism before seeking exile in the USA, where they developed influential accounts of the persuasive power of media in general, including news media, as propaganda. As an offshoot of social investigation, this approach was quickly subsumed into debates on mass media in general.

THE BRITISH RESPONSE

There was a slow but growing interest from the 1930s in the social and political implications of journalism which began to permeate British academic circles. This trend was most marked after the Second World War with the emergence of socially inclined critiques such as Richard Hoggart's (1958) *The Uses of Literacy* and Raymond Williams's (1958) *Culture and Society 1780–1950*. These were complemented by one of the most engaged and analytical books ever written by an ex-newspaper editor; the former editor of the *Daily Herald* Francis Williams's (1957) *Dangerous Estate*. However, it was to take most of the rest of the twentieth century for this gathering interest in journalism to be consolidated. A combination of the sort of exploration of broad media themes in the work of Canadian scholars such as Innis (1951, 1972) and McLuhan's (1962) groundbreaking work combined with the sociolinguistic work of Americans such as Hymes and Gumperz (1972) and Labov (1972), and began to find their way into the more overtly politicized British tradition which was emerging by the 1970s and which took the texts and practices of journalism as their starting point for social enquiry. This incorporation of these North American scholarly influences was not confined to the sociology of journalism: in historical research it took Joseph's (1961) magisterial *The Beginnings of the English Newspaper 1620–1660* to first prise accounts of the emergence of English newspapers out of the tradition of the Victorian historians of journalism and their heirs such as Herd (1952).

It was not until the 1970s that specific explorations of journalism in the UK start to develop an identity distinct from either their American antecedents or the dominant narratives of sociology. Most prominent among these was Stuart Hall, whose work from 1968 with the collective of the Birmingham Centre for Contemporary Cultural Studies drew upon the pioneering work of Richard Hoggart, the founder of the centre. Hall made a significant contribution to Smith's analysis of the social construction of identity through the language of popular newspapers in 1975, and Chibnall developed this approach still further with an influential social analysis of crime reporting in 1977. The main criticism of such sociological explorations was that they drifted from any engagement with journalism as a specific set of practices and tended to ignore producers and consumers and the environments of both the production and reception of journalism. Yet such criticism is incorporated into increasingly sophisticated analyses. For example, what starts as a series of investigations, notably from the Glasgow Media Group founded in 1974, which highlight distortions within the representations of the news media as part of a dominant ideology, soon develops into more varied and nuanced approaches to both the content of the news media and the ethnography of the industry.

MAKING THE MOST OF CONNECTIONS

The evolution of critical approaches to journalism and the appearance of the subject in a university context were both accompanied by moments of cautious welcome from high-level practitioners in the journalism industries themselves. This was seen in the appointment of senior journalists to academic roles, the appearance of senior editors at the launches of new departments or in their endorsement in taking up of positions as visiting lecturers, guest speakers or keynote lecturers at Journalism Studies conferences. These developments were important in boosting the standing of courses and their content to prospective students, those still in the industry and to university top tables. Top names on board were an indicator, albeit tenuous at times, that these new courses knew what they were doing and were often the first indicator to students that departments were informed by insider perspectives as well as the more traditional critical ones. The appointment of former senior journalists was, if nothing else, an attractive marketing ploy for many institutions. It is perhaps worth noting some of the earliest senior appointments and how this tendency has been maintained.

Hugh Stephenson, former City editor of *The Times* and editor of the *New Statesman*, was the first at City University, from 1986. Peter Cole, former deputy editor of the *Guardian* and editor of the *Sunday Correspondent*, followed at the Polytechnic of Central Lancashire in 1991. This was followed by the appointment of Donald Trelford, the former editor of the *Observer*, when he occupied the inaugural chair of Journalism Studies at the Russell Group University of Sheffield in 1994. The temptation to appoint and the willingness to accept such offers continue, as demonstrated by Tim Luckhurst of the *Scotsman* at the University of Kent and Brian Cathcart at Kingston University. There has been a developing tradition at Cardiff University of awarding professorships to senior journalists, such as Ian Hargreaves, former Director of News and Current Affairs at the BBC and former editor of the *Independent*, and Richard Tait, who combines editorial experience at the BBC with his work as Editor-in-Chief of Channel 4 News. The Journalism department at City University is full of notable journalists, including former editor of the *Daily Mirror*, Roy Greenslade. Other universities have taken to appointing honorary professors, such as Channel 4's news anchor Jon Snow at the University of Stirling, and honorary doctorates to veteran radical journalist John Pilger at the University of Lincoln. Keynote speakers to prestigious conferences are also increasingly drawn from the news media to universities, as Cardiff has demonstrated with former editor of the *Guardian* Peter Preston in 2007 at the 'Future of Newspapers' conference, and current editor of the same newspaper, Alan Rusbridger, at Sheffield in 2005 to celebrate the centenary of the university's founding charter. Increasingly, visits from, and the participation of, famous journalists acts as reassurance to students that personal experience is not lost in the critical atmosphere of the university setting.

As the courses expanded at university level, so too did published material to serve them. Franklin has observed that, with the exception of Brian McNair's book *News and Journalism in the UK*, first published in 1994, there was hardly a book published with the 'J' word in its title for decades. How different the situation is now, with a whole range of books and book series featuring 'journalism' in their titles. Publishers began to diversify from their traditional media and communication studies lists into specific sections on journalism from the early 2000s. This trend was consolidated by the publication of the book series Journalism Studies: Key Texts from Sage from 2008 onwards, which seeks to consolidate the dialogues between academy and industries in theory and practice. The increasing acceptance of Journalism Studies as a distinct area of academic enterprise was signalled when it managed to secure special subdivisional status at the prestigious USA-based International Communication Association in record time in 2006.

As journalism moved towards the status of all-graduate entry at the end of the twentieth century it became logical to expect that such a graduate profession would wish to employ graduates of journalism, and as the political drive towards the vocationalization of university education gathered pace in the early 1990s, more and more universities added journalism degrees to their undergraduate, postgraduate taught and research degree portfolios. This set up a set of challenges for journalism education in the university. First, it has to justify itself in terms of standards to its industrial overseers. This takes place amidst an escalation of economic and technological changes, which means that university education has had to respond to and prepare students for a rapidly changing industrial landscape. Within this environment, students need to demonstrate that they are flexible and critical enough to be able to respond to these changes themselves. It is no longer sufficient to receive wisdom passed on from a traditional craft tradition; students as well as their teachers have had to reflect upon the changing status and meaning of journalism in the present. All that was solid is melting into air. Second, it has to justify itself in terms of research and reflection like any other subject within the universities' expanding curricula. This combination of locating journalism study in the university system at a time of increasing challenge to the very fabric of journalism meant that journalism itself was becoming more self-reflexive than at any point in its history. The processes to which journalism contributes, and its patterns of ownership, regulation and production, even questions of whether journalism is an outmoded form of communication in the age of the blogger and the twitterer, have become major issues for debate. The time for Journalism Studies had come of age!

RESEARCH AND PUBLICATIONS

The launch of undergraduate degrees across Britain in the 1990s saw the crystallization of research and teaching specifically geared towards journalism as a subject in its own right. This included discussion and application of what might be the best ways to infuse the teaching of journalism as an academic discipline with research conducted into its practice. The use of the word 'studies' applied to journalism was an attempt to differentiate an approach to the subject from the mere passing on of a craft tradition which had become common in some institutions. Despite the fact that many courses are simply named Journalism, their combination of reflection and practical training demonstrates that they are still as much a part of the Journalism Studies tradition as those which bear that name.

The arrival of two journals specifically geared towards the new subject area in 2000, *Journalism Studies* and *Journalism: Theory, Practice and Criticism*, from two of the academic publishing world's heavyweights, Routledge and Sage, was a sign of increasing acceptance of the validity of academic studies of journalism. These subject-specific, peer-reviewed journals succeeded to a large extent in bringing professional practice and scholarly critique into reflective dialogue. Qualitative as well as quantitative pieces, empirical as well as philosophical, are found in their pages together with a range of national and globalized perspectives. They aim to be as theoretically inclusive and as methodologically diverse as befits such a multi-disciplinary set of enterprises as journalism. They have been particularly incisive in their ability to consider debates on the rapid commercial and technological changes facing all forms of journalism in the present, allowing journalism to take an empirical look at its own practice amidst the flux of challenge, surely a worthwhile result in itself.

THE 'INTERPRETIVE COMMUNITY'

Clearly there are still disagreements as to what Journalism Studies teaches, how it conducts its research and most pertinently how it engages with the practice and the practitioners of journalism. At times these disagreements can generate a degree of hostility from within either the news media or academic circles, yet, at its best, Journalism Studies has managed to draw these perspectives together, if not in reconciliation then at least in productive argument. We will endeavour to point readers to moments in the brief lifespan of this subject area where such disagreement has occurred.

Journalism Studies addresses those who want to understand and maybe even produce journalism as part of the broader media environment. Beyond this, it can contribute to the development of a more socially aware consumer, a more engaged citizen of the mediasphere of the twenty-first century, one who is aware that journalism is both commercial product and conduit for investigation and activism. This sort of media literacy is a hitherto under-developed aspect of the subject area and one, therefore, ripe for exploration as Journalism Studies moves towards its next phase.

Journalism Studies is ultimately an attempt to assert the importance of journalism by exploring its mechanics and its impact, in negotiation with its producers, its products and its audiences. Journalism Studies is an 'interpretive community', to borrow a term from Stanley Fish (1976). It may not be a fully formed one, nor may we want it to become one for fear of it becoming static and stale, but it is a community nevertheless. It is full of argument and dissent but mostly of a collegial if not a convivial nature. It currently has no 'canon' and is consequently a remarkably energetic, diverse and dynamic environment. Beware anyone who tells you the answer to the question 'What is Journalism Studies?' is a simple one because journalism is at heart a simple practice. It isn't. It's much more interesting than that!

FURTHER READING

Allan (1999) *News Culture Open*, Open University Press, is a wide-ranging introduction into the products and practices of contemporary journalism, and his later edited collection (2005) *Journalism: Critical Issues*, Open University Press, produces a fine range of polemical writing on the subject from a range of top contributors.

Allan (2009) *The Routledge Companion to News and Journalism*, Routledge – all 704 pages of it! – takes the reader on a rich journey from discussion of the ideals of journalism, through its routines and processes to its possible future. Its contributors provide a roll-call of many of the world's leading commentators in Journalism Studies.

Curran and Seaton (1981) have written probably the best and certainly most widely read introduction to British journalism from a historical perspective. It is now in its seventh edition and retitled to reflect the changing technological environment: (2009). *Power without Responsibility: Press, broadcasting and the internet in Britain*, Routledge.

Carter, Allan and Branston (1998) *News, Gender and Power*, Routledge, is an edited collection of observations and analysis on the broad political implications of the gendered nature of contemporary journalism.

Cole and Harcup (2009) *Newspaper Journalism*, Sage, provides a characteristically well-oiled account of the intersections of print journalism with critical commentary. It does a persuasive job of demonstrating how the future of this most traditional format may not be in terminal decline after all.

Conboy (2011) *Journalism in Britain: A historical introduction*, Sage, is an attempt to provide a primer in historical literacy for those wanting to understand why we have the news media we do.

Crisell and Starkey (2009) *Radio Journalism*, Sage, does an excellent job in maintaining a balance between assessments of the medium's adaptation to change while asserting that it is well placed to become the most prominent of future media for journalism. It is a wide-ranging account of how this form of journalism developed, what makes it distinctive and how it has negotiated changing economic and political circumstances.

Engel (1996) *Tickle the Public: One hundred years of the popular press*, Gollancz, is a tour-de-force exploring the varied and ambivalent attractions of the popular press in Britain over a hundred-year period.

Franklin (1997) *Newszack and News Media*, Routledge, provides one of the best early accounts of the shift in news values across all news media platforms and is enriched by its historical context, empirical observations and witty interventions on the state of journalism.

Hampton's (2004) *Visions of the Press in Britain 1850–1950*, University of Illinois Press, gives a full account of the debate over the meaning and influence of journalism in Britain over a period of a hundred years.

Harcup (2004) *Journalism: Principles and practice*, Sage, is for many the ultimate combination of practical introduction and critical commentary on contemporary journalism. It is now in its second edition (2009).

Hartley (1982) *Understanding News*, Methuen, is an early but seminal piece of analysis on the meanings of news and in particular an original contribution to how the images of television journalism function.

Greenslade (2003) *Press Gang: How newspapers make profits from propaganda*, Macmillan, is the consummate insider's view, incorporating much in the way of critical commentary and an impressive level of even-handedness in dealing with the noble as well as the ignoble aspects of newspapers.

Keeble (2005) *Print Journalism: A critical introduction*, Routledge, gathers a fine selection of leading academics and journalists to explore various features which make up historical and contemporary aspects of the wide range of styles of print journalism.

King and Chapman (2012) *Key Readings in Journalism*, Routledge, is an unusual but very welcome Anglo-American collaboration, exploring forty essential readings which reflect upon the history and social importance of journalism, prominent exponents and institutions, as well as the state of the contemporary practice and provide reflections on its future.

McNair provided the first (1994) and in many ways most influential of early assessments of the relationship between academic studies of journalism and the views of its practitioners in *News and Journalism in the UK*, Routledge. This is now in its fifth edition (2009).

Marr (2004) *My Trade: A short history of British journalism*, Pan Macmillan, is a prominent journalist's account of the debates on the nature of journalism which includes some insights into its critical reception.

Niblock (2010) *Journalism: A beginner's guide*, One World, is a good introduction to contemporary journalism, written by a 'reflexive practitioner'. A must-read for anyone thinking about studying the subject at university.

Zelizer (2004) *Taking Journalism Seriously: News and the academy*, Sage, is a fine account of the development of academic studies of journalism, almost a who's who of research into journalism combined with a polemic plea to attend to the importance of journalism as political and cultural force, from a former US journalist turned academic who is well placed to make the arguments presented here.

2

EDUCATION AND TRAINING
BETWEEN A HACK AND A HARD PLACE

INTRODUCTION

At first sight, this appears to be a straightforward chapter title, yet this combination of education and training continues to be a source of much discussion, even argument. At its heart are strongly held concerns for the content and emphasis within the process of journalism teaching. This chapter will explore the often uncomfortable stand-off between the institutions and traditions of journalism and the ways in which journalists have been prepared for their work. This preparation has often been polarized as either a skills-based training or an educational process. To counter this tendency, Journalism Studies is, at its most ambitious, an attempt to integrate the necessary skills with wider reflections on the nature and importance of journalism from both social and political perspectives. It demands of its students 'Why ask that question?' 'Why point the camera there?' 'Why choose this word not that word?' 'Will this report annoy somebody?' 'Why does journalism matter?' 'Do we care what people think of journalism?' 'How did we get here?'

This chapter will track the ways that journalism education has contributed to discussions of the nature of journalism and how attempts, both successful and unsuccessful, to professionalize it have formed part of its character. Journalism has always required at least some form of induction into what is a particular set of communication styles but this has ranged from extremely informal to tightly controlled, with varying degrees of reflection built in. This chapter will chart the development of journalism education in the UK from the informality of what was referred to as 'sitting with Nellie' to the growth of university-level education. 'Sitting with Nellie' (Allen, 2005) was the process through which a beginner would learn by watching what was done and how it was done, a largely passive and conservative practice but, as they say, it worked! We will chart the shifts in thinking on how best to prepare entrants to journalism which lay behind the development of university-level education. Amidst such discussion, it is often forgotten that it was the widespread and genuine public concern about the poor quality of journalism in the 1930s which led to recommendations designed to remedy the situation in the First Royal Commission on the Press in 1949. The motivation behind the Commission sought but ultimately failed to formalize the level and standard of journalism education. This indicates that, far from being an altruistic gesture from concerned journalists towards the improvement of standards, it was rather more exercised by anxiety that newspapers were not fulfilling the basic social and political expectations of many of their readers.

THE AMERICAN EXPERIENCE

Despite the existence of university-level education in other Anglophone countries, notably the USA, for most of the twentieth century the development of degrees at both undergraduate and postgraduate level in the UK has been a much slower process. However, even the foundation of the Journalism School at Columbia University in New York in 1908, often cited as one of the main breakthroughs for formal journalism education, was not without problem along with the opening of the University of Missouri's journalism school in the same year. The subject immediately distanced itself from a rather hostile reception with academia and it took many decades until journalism was drawn, again not unproblematically, into the orbit of cognate disciplinary areas such as mass media and communication studies. Although the curricula of North American schools could demonstrate that they provided the practical requirements for a level of proficiency in the variety of skills considered necessary to become a journalist, it was the broader social functions of journalism in the United States from the 1930s which drew deeper considerations. These were led by Park and Lippmann as pioneers in the sociological study of the interrelationship of mass communication and public political opinion.

A VERY COMPLEX PRACTICE: HISTORICAL ROOTS

First, it must be said that educating journalists is necessarily problematic given the complexity and contradiction often encapsulated in the practice of journalism itself. This is best understood if we consider the way that journalism emerged historically. Before the introduction of printed periodicals in the British Isles at the start of the seventeenth century, groups of poorly paid but literate scribes had been paid piecemeal to write out copies of letters, reports and any other documentation which were considered of interest to wealthy subscribers. They would receive the handwritten collection of latest information as a newsletter. The people who made most money out of this were not the scribes but rather those with the social and political connections which enabled them to elicit high-quality information and who had, in addition, access to a wide and wealthy network of recipients. The scribes were far from being highly prized employees and their only education consisted in having been taught to read and write. These skills, nevertheless, needed to be supplemented by a modicum of discretion, given the sensitive nature of some of the information which would have passed through their hands and before their eyes. The development of printing required a slight realignment to these patterns of production and distribution but it still meant that the printer held the power. The printer's prime motivation may have been a need to turn a profit but this could sometimes be allied to strong religious or political convictions. In fact, it was the largely Puritan printing trade which had driven much of the religious and political radicalism that swept aside the dominance of the Catholic hierarchy across Europe during the Reformation. Printing meant that the writers were now in a slightly more autonomous position than their scribe predecessors had been, as they were expected to find material and supply it to the printers on an increasingly regular basis. This meant that an ability to find reliable sources of information, and to deliver to the printers material which was considered worth printing, became important additional skills.

The torrent of publications which emerged from the years of the English Civil War (1642–9), when most formal attempts to control printing proved to be ineffective, was a demonstration of how a little political knowledge, an ability to draw upon a sound network of sources and compose quickly and to purpose could be combined to great political and commercial effect. One of the most famous periodical writers of these years, Marchamount Nedham, not only fulfilled all of the technical requirements to be described as the first English journalist, he also showed a keen understanding of the professional pragmatism necessary for survival as he changed allegiances between Parliamentarian and Royalist news publications. Nedham, however, was more educated editor than lowly hack and, as the excesses of the Civil War subsided, it continued to be the older relationship between printer and writer which defined how journalism evolved over the next few hundred years.

A SPECTRUM OF SKILLS

Two of the most widely published and best known late-seventeenth-century Grub Street writers, Tom Brown and Ned Ward, indicate something of the problem when assessing how one could become a professional periodical writer in the seventeenth and eighteenth centuries (Pinkus, 1968). Grub Street itself is the source of much of the mythologizing of journalism. It was the symbolic heart of a practice which was driven by the need to earn a living and the lucrative embarrassment which could be caused by digging up a story which would expose wrong-doing in high places. These twin demands took writers into circles which could best be described as potentially compromising to both their health and their reputations. Both authors were prolific and varied in their output, yet they were as distinguishable from their amateur gentlemanly rivals, the political pamphleteers with their powerful patrons, as they were from each other in their backgrounds. Brown was an Oxford-educated man who had aspirations to enter the Church before turning to a life of writing, while Ward was a self-taught man of humble origins. What they shared, however, was characteristic of one end of the journalism spectrum.

The other end of the market was inhabited by writers who were politically motivated and published their own periodicals to publicize these motivations or else sought political patronage to support their writerly ways. Nathaniel Mist, the owner and chief contributor to *Mist's Weekly Journal* from 1725, was an example of the former category, a Jacobite wordsmith whose political polemic saw him forced to retreat to self-imposed exile in France. Daniel Defoe, Jonathan Swift, Joseph Addison and Richard Steele were a cluster of periodical writers in the early eighteenth century whose innovations and style have brought them much celebrity in the annals of journalism. They were typical of the category of writer who sought patronage. In addition to these, some of the most powerful contributors to journals of the eighteenth century were not full-time, professional writers but letter-writers who used the periodical press to gain notoriety. Most used fictitious names to protect their identities and, in a censorious age, maintain their freedom. The work of the public writer therefore required nothing apart from skill and the ability to adapt to circumstances, both political and economic. There was no professional ethic at this point. What did exist was a great deal of antipathy between the gentleman writer, sponsored by powerful patrons, and the 'hack' whose pen was for hire to pay the rent. This dichotomy is important in considering the ways in which the education and self-perception of journalists have developed.

SOCIAL STANDING AND POLITICAL IMPACT

Paradoxically, during the eighteenth and nineteenth centuries, the professional periodical writer was nothing like as prestigious as the product of his or, more unusually, her labour. Public communication was increasingly seen as a political benefit within a democratic society, while in contrast those who provided this information for the public were often considered as the lowest of the low, disreputable types with no scruples. In terms of training and prestige, it was the printer who had to submit to a formal apprenticeship and made handsome, regular profits if successful, while the writer could be hired and fired on a daily basis. It is a historical irony that, as journalism was approaching the peak of its reputation as a stormer of the bastions of the mighty and privileged, when it was wrestling with the State to ensure its ability to write freely without fear of redress and to report the proceedings of democratically elected representatives in Parliament, the people who produced the routine content of newspapers were considered an abject, unkempt and unreliable breed, the hacks of Grub Street! Yet the contradiction between the esteem in which information was held and the purveyors of that same information has a rational explanation. The independence of the 'hack' from the whip of political favour depended upon the financial independence of the early journalists and, although this often meant that the journalists trod a precarious economic tightrope, it was something that they were stubbornly proud of. Samuel Johnson had summed up all the bitter acceptance of this necessity as early as 1776, when he was reported as saying:

No man but a blockhead wrote, except for money.

WHAT KIND OF JOURNALISM?

The social and political standing of journalists and debates about the need for them to be formally educated or not are a direct consequence of the wide range and ambition of the work that a journalist might produce. By the nineteenth century there were at least five different layers of journalist, an observation which makes the assessment of what might have been a suitable education or training for them an even more complex process. There was the radical pamphleteer, a publicist who had no regard for anything other than the dissemination of his particular position on contemporary events and the proclamation of solutions to his readers. These also doubled up as public performers at political meetings and their prose reflected the cadences of oral delivery required in such environments. Writers who fitted into this mould included Thomas Paine, acknowledged radical proponent of both the American and French Revolutions, whose pamphlets sold in their hundreds of thousands and which were credited with altering the course of political history, and William Cobbett, a convert to a solid English radicalism, whose work highlighted the exploitation of the poor rural stock of England by a corrupt and idle aristocracy. Patriotic and polemical, he produced his weekly *Political Register* (1802–35) and toured the country addressing assemblies in support of parliamentary reform. Second, there were gentlemen editors such as James Perry of the *Morning Chronicle* (1789–1817), or John Delane, editor of the *Times* (1841–77), who enabled their respective newspapers to become enlightened contributors to the culture and politics of their age, albeit more through their judicious appointments of talented contributors than by the energies of their own writing. Third, there were the essayists and novelists such as William Hazlitt (1788–1830) and Charles Dickens (1812–70), who plied literary careers at the same time as they contributed to the more transient world of journalism. Fourth, there were the commercial populists who had the ear and the eye of the masses as well as a well-developed understanding of how to encourage them to buy their products. They could organize periodicals to capture the attention of the crowd and went on to earn fortunes out of popular journalism. Prominent among them in the late nineteenth century were George Newnes and Alfred Harmsworth, famous respectively for the publication of *Tit-Bits* (1881) and the *Daily Mail* (1896). Fifth, and finally, there were the lowly producers of routine reports, poorly paid and unattributed, lost to history in their anonymity. This group included the 'penny-a-liners' – often women – who were not allowed to leave the premises to ply their trade, who were hired and fired at a moment's notice and who claimed little in the way of literary skill. Their work was similar in its lowly status to that of the scriveners of the pre-printing era, making them the sweatshop scribes of the industrial age. Such a diversity in both the types of work and the workers themselves meant that it was completely understandable that no real consensus emerged about the best preparation for a job in journalism. It was simply too varied.

As the nineteenth century progressed we see more of an emphasis on the reporting of the world than on the dissemination of political opinion as journalism moved towards a more systematic set of practices and more of a professionally organized and capitalized industry. Nevertheless, the need for those at the bottom with a little literary ability and an ability to forage for news, as well as those at the top with the right social background and a ruthless business acumen, still remained. How one was educated to enter such employment depended on what sort of journalist you wanted to be.

THE QUESTION OF PROFESSIONALISM

James Cameron, in response to the growing literature on journalism, is quoted in the *Journalism Reader*:

> Journalism is not and never has been a profession; it is a trade, or a calling, that can be practised in many ways, but it can never be a profession since its practice has neither standards nor sanctions ... This may well be a good thing, since while this flexibility and permissiveness gives entry to a number of dubious oddballs it equally does not exclude many valuable and original people.
>
> (Cameron, 1997: 170)

The question of how best to educate journalists is complicated, partly as a consequence of the industrialization of journalism over the nineteenth century and also on account of the long and related story of the flawed attempts to professionalize it. As journalism flourished in the second half of the nineteenth century its profitability drew in investment and advertising, and the newspaper became increasingly segmented into different specialized roles and activities. At the same time, it was presented as a vital component of the democratic system, thereby, apparently, elevating its practitioners to an important political function somewhat at odds with their lowly social and economic status. To reconcile this contradiction between status and function, journalists began to organize themselves and militate for better recognition. They pursued this in two ways: professionalization and unionization.

Throughout the Victorian period, occupations such as science, medicine, law and education strove to be recognized as professions and sought to establish both the reputation and social standing of their practitioners by carefully controlling entry and monitoring standards of behaviour. However, these practices were also subtly designed to keep out those who did not conform to the Victorian ideal of the upper-middle-class gentleman, such as women and the working classes. This meant that professionalization became a means of increasing status by exclusion, as well as enhancing claims that this sort of gendered and social exclusivity added to the reputation of the particular professionalizing occupations. Professions kept out undesirables! Journalism posed problems for this model as it was an occupation which was increasingly targeted towards women in both its magazine and popular newspaper forms and unsurprisingly therefore it was employing more women to write material of interest to this audience. A further problem lay in the fact, discussed above, that journalism would draw upon anybody who had a story to tell and could write it in a manner which matched the style and pleased the readers of a particular publication. Journalism had never been fussy about who it employed and nobody could be excluded from contributing because they were not acceptable to a small clique of self-protecting insiders. A writer could simply take his or her work elsewhere in the marketplace of print and, since this was often concentrated around one particular part of central London, a new employer could be found a few minutes' walk or a few drinks away. Such marginal status as the periodical writer enjoyed was indeed an advantage for writers looking for work at a time when journalism started to become more interested in presenting material in as entertaining a fashion as possible and in the ability of a new generation of reporters to uncover information and even scandal of interest to a popular audience. Influences from the practices of popular journalism in the USA included the increasingly aggressive assertion of reporters that they had the right to go wherever was necessary and ruffle as many feathers as required to uncover the truth. This influx of the traditions of 'aggression and access' from American journalism, notably after the American Civil War (1861–5), was not at all in keeping with the self-styled decorum and prestige of the new Victorian professions. Muckraking was nevertheless good business.

COLLECTIVE IDENTITY AND UNIONIZATION

As a solution to this inability to identify much in the way of a professional tradition, journalists took the other route open to workers who wish to establish a collective identity as a form of protection against unscrupulous employers and to promote their own contribution to social and political life. This second route was unionization. Yet the journalists' approach had a strange institutional beginning, as the first national organization which attempted to rally journalists to common cause was set up by the newspaper owners as the National Association of Journalists in 1886. Its respectability was underlined by its receipt of a Royal Charter as it changed its name to the Institute of Journalists in 1890. The Institute identified some of the issues which, if addressed, could have enabled journalism to begin to consider itself a profession as defined at the time. It argued for improved conditions of employment for journalists being matched by a better preliminary education for its members and, although it wished in principle to impose a level of entry qualification, as was the case for medicine or law, for example, it could not settle upon any final set of tests which could assess an aptitude for the potential range of activities which had come to characterize journalism. It continued in its efforts to identify how best to restrict entry to journalism to those who could meet the demands of the owners of newspapers well into the 1930s, when it twice sponsored a Journalists' Registration Bill in Parliament, but these attempts failed to become established as law.

In 1907 the National Union of Journalists was founded, as proof that there was considerable support from journalists for an organization which would differentiate itself from the demands of employers and which could address the issues common to most trades unions, those of pay and conditions for their membership. In fact, its first task was to attempt to establish binding minimum wages for different categories of journalist. This union route to occupational identity, however, ran contrary to that established by those seeking for journalism to be considered a profession, Moreover, the ways that journalism recruited and remunerated its employees made the establishment of a 'going rate' for the job highly problematic. Specialist reporters, notably theatre and literary reviewers, were much more likely to be able to negotiate their own fees as part of a portfolio of employment without being tied down to a fixed rate or even a contract. They would gravitate to wherever their expertise and contacts would be best rewarded. Political insiders were more likely to be gentlemen with similar backgrounds to the politicians themselves, with access to the same clubs and social circles. To these men, fixed rates, contracts and unions would have been an unnecessary and even unsavoury intrusion into their own perceptions of their working practices.

Anybody with a story to sell and the ability to write it could be paid as a freelance in the expanding market for popular news and magazines from the late Victorian period onwards. To compound this, throughout the twentieth century the opportunities increased for a journalist to become a named, celebrity columnist with salaries that matched his/her fame and attractiveness to newspaper and magazine owners. All these aspects conspired against any generalized collective approach to wages, although it did work for regular staff members to an extent. However, discussions of the nature of the journalist's work had, by the twentieth century, rather lost sight of one of the fundamental claims of journalism which differentiated it from many other occupations: its communicative role in informing democratic life. This had been relegated, particularly within print journalism, as contrasted to its later broadcast variant, by the crudest assessment of the laws of the market. If it sold, it was included. To be fair, the NUJ in its concerns over standards, ethics and the power of owners has played a part in maintaining journalism's democratic credentials, especially from 1936 in its pioneering Code of Professional Conduct. Since this point it has continued in its attempts to harness, at least, if not merge, the roles of traditional trade union and professional organization.

THE FAILURE OF PROFESSIONALIZATION

From 1927, the BBC offered a different model of professionalization distinct from the parameters of discussion within print journalism. As it was statutorily obliged to adhere to strict standards of balance and impartiality, and because of the more stable employment patterns within radio and later television journalism, a more robust alternative model of journalistic professionalism emerged. This was certainly the case until at least the 1980s, when the standards built up over the years came under attack from the forces of deregulation applied to the media environment in general by the Conservative government. However, at no point did the BBC seek to move towards one of the requirements of other professions in their insistence on specific standards of entry. In this regard, broadcasting remained ultimately as 'unprofessionalized' as any other branch of journalism.

Despite the exceptionalism of the BBC, during the 1960s and 1970s, a period which saw widespread professionalization in employment practices in Britain, an influential survey (Tunstall, 1971) concluded that journalism still did not fulfil the majority of criteria which were widely considered as constituting a modern profession. As can be imagined, if this was the situation at the highpoint of 'professionalization' in the modern era, it is not at all surprising that by the 1990s, after waves of anti-trade union legislation, assaults on employment security and the unfettered role of the market as a part of neo-liberal solutions to the introduction of new technologies to the workplace, most of the strategies attempting to professionalize journalism had been suspended or even eradicated. The widespread derecognition of trade unions by employers, the rise of what have been identified as macho management styles, the elevation of the bottom line of profit above almost everything else and the increase in contracts negotiated individually all conspired to erode the progress made towards professionalization in journalism, in ways which benefited the interests of the corporate owners of news media. All of these trends intensified after the move of Murdoch's News International to its purpose-built new premises in Wapping in 1986, and most had become common practice, encouraged by Murdoch's success, within a very short space of time across Britain's news media.

RESIDUAL TENDENCIES

The NUJ is still active in campaigning for a better expression of the roles and responsibilities of journalism across the board, including its monitoring of the adherence of journalists to its Code of Conduct and the work of its Ethics Council. This comes despite the decrease in its membership which has come as a consequence of fragmenting employment patterns and the hostility to collective organization from employers. It is highly supportive of journalism education at universities and recognizes courses without getting involved in issues of accreditation or regulation. It provides speakers and enrols students as student members of the NUJ, encouraging them to adhere to the Code of Conduct throughout their studies.

Broadcast journalism in the UK, on account of its more regulated nature and its statutory commitments to impartiality and refraining from editorializing, has always trodden a different path with regards to professionalism. Although, by and large, the broadcasters have kept out of discussions on the best ways to educate journalists, being content to assume that journalists will have experience in print journalism and general news procedures before applying for a job as a radio or television journalist, they are bound to more professionalized standards of editorial control. The BBC in particular remains highly unionized, as demonstrated in the NUJ's recent success there in negotiating its members' pension provision in 2010. Its journalists see a direct correlation between the professional aspirations of collective representation and union-negotiated pay scales and career structure. They comply with both the NUJ's Code of Conduct and have adhered to the BBC's own Editorial Guidelines since 1996. On account of the fact that full-time broadcast journalism jobs are much harder to come by than posts in other news media, there is little room to manoeuvre in interpreting these guidelines and journalists stick to them as closely as possible. In fact it was the perceived inability of a BBC journalist, Andrew Gilligan, to uphold the expected standards of integrity at the BBC which led, in the wake of the Hutton Report into the death of Dr David Kelly, to the setting up in 2005 of the BBC's own College of Journalism, which is an explicit attempt to revitalize professional commitment to the highest standards at the BBC through the education and training of its journalists. To a large extent, this has formalized its preparation of journalists.

The contrast of responsible broadcast journalists, in both independent and public service broadcasting, with those in disreputable and 'edgy' print media, especially at the popular tabloid end of the scale, continues, although somewhat paradoxically the BBC's own journalists are happy to retreat to the position that theirs is a scurrilous trade despite the institution's own high principles. Andrew Marr's (2004) influential pronouncement in 2004 on its being a craft or trade, not a profession, still remains problematic if journalism wishes to pronounce itself as a constituent of the democratic good. In one respect Marr is right. He roots his 'trade' historically and it is within such a context that we need to study its development. However, Kevin Marsh, former editor of BBC Radio 4's *Today* programme, provided a view of his industry in which he articulated his anxieties for its future, especially if it could not address public concerns about its self-image, in a speech to the Society of Newspaper Editors in October 2004:

> Journalists are members of Britain's least trusted profession: the press. More than 90 per cent of the population trust their doctor to tell the

truth; less than a fifth trust the press to do the same. It's not an essential condition of journalism. Trust in broadcasters is very much higher and trust in the BBC higher still ... Government ministers and MPs share the lowly standing of the press – we don't trust those we've chosen to exercise power for us; and we don't trust those who tell us how the chosen are doing it ... The crisis of trust cannot be any great surprise to anyone. Why should anyone trust a practitioner of any craft or profession who doesn't seem to know and is unable or unwilling to articulate what that craft or profession is for? Or who wears indifference to the effects of that craft as a badge of honour? Or who seems to relish denial of responsibility, playing the romantic maverick, happy to be identified only as someone who kicks against authority, just out to make trouble and get up people's noses?

(Marsh, 2004: 17)

EDUCATION AS PART OF THE PROCESS OF PROFESSIONALIZATION

Part of this long, problematic and unresolved process of professionalization has been a consideration of what sort of education was desirable for journalists. Although it is often stated that formal journalism education was established in American universities long before they gained a foothold in Britain, these courses were often disappointingly distanced from the mainstream of academic endeavour and were merely skills-based and therefore out of step with the expectations and traditions of the academy. The earliest courses were set up in Kansas, Iowa and Wisconsin as early as 1903 and Pulitzer's Columbia School of Journalism was proposed in 1908 at the same time as Walter William's School of Journalism was inaugurated at the University of Missouri. Columbia's was set up in 1910, although because of its preference for a separation from other academic faculties it had been rejected by Princeton a year or so beforehand. By 1927, Schools of Journalism within universities had developed from earlier experiments grounded in practice. In order for the subject to gain intellectual respectability, however, it needed to engage with social scientific traditions of academic enquiry and this led in the post-war era to its tracking with mass communication studies.

In Britain, there were many attempts to set up training schools but nothing at university level until a diploma course was offered at King's College between 1922 and 1939. This did not prove to be a success and it was discontinued within a few years. Journalism was not perceived as something worthy of sustained study from an academic perspective, despite its grand historical claims to be an intrinsic part of the democratic process.

STANDARDS AND STANDING

The perception that much newspaper journalism was unconcerned with anything above the bottom line of providing cheap entertainment for the masses was unfortunately confirmed in the eyes of many commentators as it embarked in the 1920s and 1930s in a ferocious series of circulation wars in which free gifts such as complete sets of encyclopedias, the works of Charles Dickens and even a free piano were offered to subscribers who could be seduced by ever more lurid displays of chequebook journalism, sensationalism and the relegation of political reporting to an afterthought. The circulation wars further consolidated the impression within the public mind that journalism, particularly national newspaper journalism, was a scurrilous practice driven by megalomaniac owners and produced by writers whose sole claim to fame was that they could deliver cliché to order.

Concern about the standards, ethics and ownership of the press, combined with the elevated reputation of the broadcast journalism of the BBC as it emerged triumphant from the Second World War, meant that the full glare of public scrutiny was targeted at newspapers in the first Royal Commission on the Press in 1947. This made a direct link between the widely acknowledged poor standards of journalism ethics and the generally low level of education for all but the most privileged of elite journalists. The Commission also took up the issue of the standards of behaviour of individual journalists and recommended the setting up of a General Council of the Press which would censure undesirable conduct and uphold the highest professional standards. This came into being as the Press Council in 1953.

One of the Commission's recommendations, designed to improve the quality and consistency of journalism education, was implemented by the setting up of the National Council for the Training of Journalists. This was initially designed as a skills-based set of qualifications which would be delivered by local colleges of further education (as a post-entry qualification). New recruits to local newspapers, the primary group targeted by the NCTJ, would be allowed day release from their employers. It was never intended to include much in the way of studying the subject of journalism in its political or cultural contexts. It did little to shift the impression of journalism training as a craft apprenticeship and nothing to professionalize journalism as a practice. There is even much anecdotal evidence that many who failed its exams went on to enjoy high-profile and successful careers in journalism. The NCTJ did construct a syllabus and a course of training in 1951 which ran in further education colleges as both pre-entry and post-entry training schemes and these were generally well received by newspapers. However, not completing such a course or even failing it outright did not automatically prevent somebody with the required skills to start working as a journalist at either a local or a national level, meaning that any attempt to use even this low-grade induction into the basics of journalism as an entry requirement to a profession were quashed from the start. Such training merely took the edge off newspapers' requirements to train new recruits on the job. It was a cost-effective way of enabling new recruits to acquire certain rudimentary skills if they needed them for their particular type of work. The main disadvantage of the NCTJ approach was that, as a skills-based model, it was inherently conservative and hardly provided adequate groundwork for the sort of reflective practice which had become the hallmark of the professions. In no way could it be considered a recipe to resolve the concerns which had led to the pre-war demise of journalism's reputation and its subsequent scrutiny by the Royal Commission, or to respond to its assumption that some formal training would in itself improve standards of newspaper journalism.

SPECIALIZATION AND EDUCATION

The second half of the twentieth century would see no let-up in the acceleration of trends away from the generalist 'hack' and towards a greater degree of specialization within journalism. Just as there was still a need for elite-educated and socially well-connected editors and senior correspondents on national newspapers, there was an increasingly wide range of functions within the newspaper from celebrity columnists, legal and financial specialists, political reporters and commentators, sports specialists, freelance specialists and generalists, editorial assistants, sub-editors and picture editors. The complexity and the variety have grown as the technological platforms for delivery have multiplied and, as unionization has declined since the late twentieth century, the traditional specializations have been added to by an army of unpaid interns.

The trend towards greater professionalization noticeable in many areas of employment in Britain by the 1960s mentioned above did encourage the development of more formal courses in journalism and as national and local newspaper groups developed their own bespoke training schemes, associations with universities started to appear. The first was at Cardiff University when the Thompson Foundation Training College linked with the university to set up a postgraduate diploma in journalism in 1970. This soon became established as an alternative to formal NCTJ local college courses. Soon afterwards City University in London founded its own Graduate Centre for Journalism in 1976.

The situation across Britain remained static until the introduction of a rapidly expanding range of new courses at postgraduate level but also for the first time at undergraduate level, often at newly established universities post-1992, with a focus on vocational training for students from backgrounds where university education had not traditionally been an expectation. This had the benefit that increasingly the entry into journalism, particularly at grassroots level, became far more transparent than ever before, potentially enabling bright working-class graduates to acquire the required skills, often – but not always – on courses accredited by the National Council for the Training of Journalists (NCTJ), the Broadcast Journalism Training Council (BJTC) or the Periodicals Training Council (PTC) to prove to editors that they could be employed ready for immediate impact on their products. This didn't mean that these wealthy and successful news media enterprises felt any more like investing any of their profits into journalism education but at least it showed that higher education was able to produce performers as competent as those who had come through the previously opaque entry channels. Even Russell Group universities, research-led and rather traditionally oriented institutions, launched undergraduate journalism degrees in the 1990s, most notably at the University of Sheffield with former *Observer* editor Donald Trelford as its inaugural head of department. By the end of the 1990s there were, according to UCAS statistics, over sixty UK institutions offering degrees badged variously as journalism or journalism studies either at undergraduate or postgraduate levels. Some of these degrees were single honours but as often as not they were offered as a combination with a wide range of other subjects. Despite criticism from some quarters of the tendency to provide dual degrees, one of the most prestigious undergraduate programmes at City University always offered its journalism in conjunction with a social science. If the possession of a degree had been a key indicator of a professional in the 1970s, then certainly journalism was following this trend, with over 70 per cent of journalists at that point possessing a degree of some sort. More recently, in the wake of the university expansion of the 1990s, figures from the Journalism Training Forum indicate that 98 per cent of new entrants have a first degree as a minimum qualification.

There are a bewildering range of courses currently on offer, including FE short courses, undergraduate single honours with and without accreditation, undergraduate joint honours without accreditation, postgraduate diplomas, postgraduate certificates, postgraduate accredited MAs and postgraduate MAs without accreditation. Although many of the graduates from these courses will find work as journalists, there is no requirement for any to have an accredited degree as a qualification and it remains perfectly acceptable for a new recruit to journalism to arrive with a qualification in some other academic or professional area. The maze of potential qualifications also varies enormously with regard to how training is balanced against broader cultural and political contextualization. Some courses merely provide a set of skills with little else. Others provide a whole range of approaches to balancing vocationalism with broader social science or humanities contributions to offer a richer background. Even the University of Oxford has entered the arena, enabled by Reuters to set up a Centre for the Study of Journalism in 2006, although it does not recruit students to study for any specific award and acts more as a think-tank for policy makers and as a sympathetic location for international journalists to spend a productive sabbatical.

THE CURRICULUM

If you are going to study journalism, then what should you 'study'? 'Study' here is quite a contested word. The study of journalism is not quite the same thing as learning a set of skills or principles. In fact, it is completely different. Clearly, journalism as a set of skills and techniques had been transmitted from one generation to another as effectively as it needed to have been in order to ensure its survival, maintaining its profitability to the owners and managers of news media. But this was not nearly enough. The legal, ethical and political anxieties, alluded to above, which relate to the content of journalism and the ability of journalists to provide the information necessary for a modern citizenship may have reached a peak by the end of the Second World War, but the timid solutions of the Royal Commissions have not brought resolution to the linkage optimistically projected between a more structured education for journalists and an improvement in the quality of journalism.

The answer to these perennial issues that has emerged in university education in the UK has been characteristically pragmatic. Courses which are named as journalism degrees clearly have to have a strongly vocational element and this needs to be backed up with technology which is as advanced as possible. You probably do not want to spend three whole years merely being inducted into a set of industrial norms, as this would mean that you could not engage critically and creatively with the possibilities of journalism. Such a restricted curriculum would also prevent you from locating journalism within its wider social and political contexts, which is what its audience does all the time whether as consumers or as concerned political actors. Universities have consequently tended to exploit their existing staffing and research expertise in order to construct syllabi which are as congruent with the practicalities of journalism as they are with the research themes within their departments. It is this combination that creates the blend of practice and reflection which forms the heart of the most prestigious degrees at both undergraduate and postgraduate level and distinguishes their students from mere button-pushers or mouse-clickers. Degrees need a full complement of applied modules which prepare students for ethical considerations and legal requirements concerning representation and libel, as well as other modules which might range from social and political reflections on the purpose and function of journalism, its literary distinctiveness, historical aspects of journalism or discussions of how journalism has engaged with various technological challenges. Sometimes these modules might be taught within the department or school of journalism or within a broader media and communications ecology; they might even be delivered as part of a joint degree with other departments or even other faculties. Whichever way is selected, the result is a great deal of variety across the higher education sector, full of choice and vitality for students as one would expect of an area of public communication characterized by its diversity and dynamism.

At undergraduate level courses tend to start with a general overview in their first year, moving to greater specialization and more scope for the pursuit of individual interests as they progress. Postgraduate courses, whether MA or diploma, because of their intensive nature tend to focus on the practical training of the skills base for employment, assuming that the intellectual skills have been provided by a good-quality undergraduate education.

The one drawback with many courses is that, vocationally driven as these courses are, they have tended up to now to be characterized by a cautious approach to the substance of journalism. This is typified by an assumption that journalists start as many did in the past on a local newspaper and need specific skills to enable them to deal with this particular environment. However, work on local newspapers is disappearing as fast as the local newspapers themselves, and the opportunity now exists for such courses to reconsider the traditional and rather conservative nature of news values, the relationships between producers and consumers, and the role of technology in the changing agendas and identities of news providers.

University departments are doing all they can to keep up with and deliver technologically relevant teaching of the practical skills as journalism's parameters shift within the digital environment. Good contacts with news media industries help departments to maintain a realistic approach to what students are likely to face on graduating if they are able to secure work as a journalist, whether full-time or freelance. They need to consider how to prepare students to work with multi-platform, multi-skilled approaches to the provision of news and to consider the problems and opportunities emerging between the work of the amateur blogger and the work of the remunerated journalist. In this way students are often in the front line of demonstrating the interaction between theory and practice, as journalism is redefined for a new generation. After all, whether journalism survives either as a practice or as a product largely depends on the decisions and activities of this generation of producers and consumers of news media. The future of journalism is in our students' hands. We should take good care of them.

BEYOND PRACTICE

Debate on the content and the disciplinary location of journalism courses has included the rather sceptical view of Kevin Williams (1999), who expressed concern about what he perceived as the lack of coherence in many of the approaches to journalism at university level. However, he remains convinced that journalism departments can produce a combination which is sympathetic to the goals of journalism and emerge as an intellectual field in its own right. De Burgh (2005) stresses the importance of journalism education going beyond the practical while insisting that the basic editorial skills remain at the heart of such a curriculum. Often these views are influenced by contemporary discussions emanating from the USA, where significant work from both academics and former journalists has been produced on how best to construct a curriculum which combines practice and research-led reflection in equal measure. One excellent example emanates from Columbia University, where Andie Tucher (2011) – a journalist turned professor – teaches a history course premised on the insight that if we know what changed in journalism in the past, and why, then we can consider what needs to change in the present. Awareness of the mutability of journalism's cultural and political contexts is a clear demonstration of the fact that journalism is not a fixed set of practices any more than any other form of cultural production.

ACCREDITATION AND CERTIFICATION

Understanding the current provision of journalism education at universities in Britain is not made any simpler by confusion caused by questions of course accreditation and approval. Some courses are accredited and there are certainly bodies which do accredit courses, such as the PTC and the BJTC. There is also a body, NCTJ, which sets examinations and monitors the content of courses taught to prepare students for these examinations. The accreditation of broadcast courses is very different, since the BJTC is a very different creature from the NCTJ. Set up in 1979 to maintain and support standards in the training of broadcast journalists it takes a much less prescriptive approach than the NCTJ. It does not set its own exams but does scrutinize the content of courses. Furthermore, it provides advice and recommendations where necessary as part of its accreditation process. The more recent Periodicals Training Council takes the view of the BJTC that it is there to advise on the standards expected but not to set the exams itself; to encourage a certain preference towards magazines in the curriculum but without prescribing course content. There are universities which run journalism courses which are approved or accredited by one or all of these organizations and there are also fine journalism courses which, while seeking accreditation from the BJTC or the PTC, avoid what they see as the overly prescriptive intrusions of the NCTJ.

RESPONSES FROM WITHIN

Despite its obvious orientation to a paying public, journalism has perhaps ironically tended to consider itself a rather closed community. Anti-social hours, professional camaraderie and a suspicion of authority, including managerial authority, combined with noble notions of the freedom of the press and its claims to constitute a 'Fourth Estate', have meant that investigations from outsiders into that community have often been met with resistance or even hostility. When journalism was dominated by men who had graduated from the school of life or had passed from school through a rough and ready system of apprenticeship into their working lives, most of the hostility was reserved for those who had attended university and especially for academics who sought to understand or appeared to want to pass judgement on what journalists did for a living. As more graduates have entered journalism, these sorts of perspective on graduates have generally disappeared but the insiders can still appear sceptical about the value of specialist journalism degrees.

There are still exceptions, however, and the generally negative tone of debates about the merits of 'media studies' within the news media themselves are characteristic of hostility to any sustained examination of the media, including the news media.

The UK has by and large avoided the savagery of the debate around journalism education which echoed around Australian universities a few years ago (Tomaselli, 2002). This seemed to create a distinction between journalism practice and critical enquiry into journalism, a divide across which neither side of the argument was able to bridge. Despite, or on account of, healthy debate between those involved in the academic analysis of journalism and those teaching how to go about doing it, including some who do both, sometimes at the same time, there is in the UK a broad consensus on the need to remain, at least, engaged in discussion. The Association for Journalism Education, as the main forum for discussions of university-level journalism education, is adamant that journalism education needs to establish the centrality of reflection within its own pedagogic practice. This entails, as exists at various institutions across the UK already, a broader acknowledgement from both former practitioners and from current journalists that journalists need to reflect on the wider debate about their own products and practices so as to enable the next generation to avoid the sort of ostrich-like response which dismisses all thinking about journalism from wider society as some sort of conspiracy.

Despite the pragmatic attempts by universities to provide as broad a choice as possible for students wishing to study journalism and to encourage them to consider careers in news media industries which can appear so dauntingly difficult to enter, the reception from those privileged to have a voice within those news media has often been less than reassuring. First, there is the frequent conflation of Journalism Studies with Media Studies. This comes despite the fact that these different courses are flagged and marketed very differently. It does make you wonder quite what the rationale for such hostility might be. It might simply be that the all-invasive media do not take kindly to being studied and analysed themselves. On a vocational level, Media Studies courses provide some of the most employable graduates in the UK according to surveys of graduate employability; on an intellectual level, Media Studies provide some of the most insightful research into the global and national media so it is an area where British students are exposed to much of the best teaching and brightest minds in the field; on a media literacy level, it would be hard to argue against the case for the value of studying such a hugely important part of our contemporary reality and equally hard to dismiss it as 'Mickey Mouse Studies'. It would be disappointing to see such prejudice displayed in any newspaper but the fact that an oft-cited and characteristic article on this topic was published in the *Independent*, a publication which has a high-profile media commentary section itself, was particularly disappointing. 'This paper regards a degree in media studies as a disqualification for the career of journalism' was published on 31 October 1996, when any discerning student had a range of choices of either media studies or journalism degrees.

Such an unwillingness to engage with the realities of contemporary journalism education can be contrasted with the responses from experienced journalists such as Tony Delano (2008), in the *British Journalism Review*, who asks colleagues to first consider the ecology of journalism education without jumping to a ill-informed opinion which reflects badly upon the industry's ability to appreciate an education with a great deal of practical and intellectual merit. The author is a veteran Fleet Street journalist who has been active in journalism education for many years and is the author of several esteemed reports and books on journalism as well as being the holder of a PhD: an unusually full row of cherries on a journalism educator's CV! He reviews the range of provision and invites fellow journalists to have more regard for the differences across the HE sector, instead of using blanket criticism, entitling his contribution 'Different horses, different courses'.

Nevertheless, these debates serve in the main to play a mostly constructive part in the process of shaping Journalism Studies and its reception within the news media industries at a time of rapid change and pragmatic reflection on what journalism can contribute to contemporary public communication.

If journalism education is to provide an adequate complement to the professionalization of journalism and generate greater opportunities for reflection on the political and cultural importance of journalism as it is actually practised, as opposed to how it is idealized, then it needs journalism itself to get out more among its critics, including its consumers. If journalism education is to be able to do its work of professionalizing and socializing the next generations of journalists, it needs to be further encouraged from within the news media industry and these media themselves need to be aware of debates among critics outside their practice, critics who are often consumers or citizens concerned about the content and the preparation of practitioners for this important work. Journalist educators might well agree that a journalism syllabus needs to start with expectations of citizens and consumers as a first port of call rather than merely accepting that journalism is an exclusively market-driven process which answers automatically to the call of a contemporary neo-liberal consensus: the market. Maybe journalism education needs to start at the entry level with higher expectations and lay greater emphasis on critique, even within its preparation for the practical elements of journalism.

As an experienced journalist and journalism educator from the USA has put it (Glasser, 2006), journalism education needs to move beyond the clichés and platitudes that newsrooms use to ward off critics. Such an excavation can lead students to understand how current practices have emerged and whose interests they may or may not serve. At least then they would be going into journalism with their eyes open! A rounded journalism education can and does provide students at many universities with skills and training, but skills and training plus. It can also do much to provide the additional context for future practitioners to operate reflectively and critically within society's wider expectations. In part this is provided by essential engagement in formal teaching of ethics and law but these aspects of the curriculum need to be aligned with broader concerns of how journalism fits into critical perspectives of journalism, its functions and its failings. Future journalists need to be critical, because their audience is itself increasingly critical to the extent that many are no longer buying the products of journalism or they are themselves sceptical about what distinguishes a journalist from a blogger, an amateur citizen-journalist from an accredited professional. It is for the coming generation of journalists to demonstrate the continuing contribution of journalism to society. A fully rounded journalism education at university should aim to produce practitioners who can robustly defend the integrity of journalism in the face of a new generation of citizen-consumers. To achieve this, they need to be equipped with a broad knowledge of the contemporary challenges and critiques facing the practice.

THE ASSOCIATION FOR JOURNALISM EDUCATION

There has been an educational movement emerging out of the establishment of journalism as an academic subject. Working in largely unnavigated waters within an institutional framework often lacking understanding of what journalism education might aspire to in a university setting, former journalists and academics drawn into the subject area needed to establish their own network of information and strategy. They set up a forum for professional debate which became institutionalized as the Association for Journalism Education in 1997. Its website (http://www.ajeuk.org/) asserts that its aims are to uphold the highest standards in journalism education; to provide a common voice for those involved in it; to promote and support research into journalism education and journalism more generally. This association regularly organizes conferences and seminars to consider developments within the news media industry, how these can be reflected in the curricula at university and how good-quality research can enhance the teaching of journalism and its cultural contexts. The AJE is particularly concerned to maintain the vocational, experiential aspects of journalism in its academic setting as well as to encourage former journalists to become more active in the full range of academic activities associated with universities, such as publication, peer-review and research funding applications. It has over fifty paid-up member institutions and hundreds of active participants, and has begun to participate formally in global discussions of the roles and responsibilities of journalism education in differing geo-political environments. It was in fact the AJE which commissioned the most up-to-date research into journalism education in the UK by Delano and published by the professional journal the *British Journalism Review* in 2008 (mentioned above). In fact, it regularly advertises generous bursaries for such work. It is currently launching its latest intervention in the form of an ambitious online peer-reviewed journal, to be launched from 2012, entitled *Journalism Education*.

ENGAGING WITH NEW TECHNOLOGIES

Journalism education is having to engage on a regular basis with the realities of the changing technological environment of journalism itself. The ease with which one can publicize one's thoughts and opinions, and even what is happening in your world without formal training or certification, does beg the question whether journalism education has anything specific to offer the next generation. The robust response of university departments has been not only to equip themselves with the latest equipment and software but perhaps more importantly to emphasize the difference between a fully reflective practice responsible to the public, engaging with public concerns about standards and the amateur and sometimes irresponsible enthusiasms of the social media networks no matter how dynamic and innovative they might be. Journalism departments have had their minds focused by technological innovation to assertions that journalism is no longer an identifiable practice within the fragmenting media landscape and have consequently had to revitalize their teaching and their research to be able to distinguish between technology and technique for a new generation. Working within this environment and with the latest technologies, students are learning more about what continues to make journalism distinctive as a communication form. It is highly unlikely that such a rich pool of talent, equipped as they are to deal with the demands of this new era for journalism, could be produced were it not for the institutional efforts of those working within Journalism Studies, and more broadly journalism education, in the university sector today.

EDUCATION: ENGAGING WITH INEQUALITIES

The education of journalists has also been used to highlight but not resolve issues about the social and ethnic composition of journalism. It was once the preserve of mainly lower-middle-class white men. This has changed, but not much. Beulah Ainley, a freelance journalist and educator, interviewed over one hundred journalists from Afro-Caribbean and Asian backgrounds with experience of working in newspapers, television and radio for his book *Black Journalists, White Media*. The book makes striking links between the under-representation of black journalists in the predominantly white media to practices of direct and indirect discrimination. Furthermore he demonstrates the weakness of the NUJ in particular in putting positive-action equal opportunities into place. A Society of Editors' report from 2004 entitled *Diversity in the Newsroom* exposed how little genuine diversity is to be found even on local newspapers serving local communities which include large ethnic minorities. This gives the lie to the common assertion that local newspapers prefer to employ people who know their community and demonstrates instead that much needs to be done if a more representative balance is ever going to be able to capture a better representation from within the local community in employment terms. This is particularly relevant to local newspapers, of course, as it is their profit-base which has been slashed by the flight of small advertising from the local press to online alternatives. Stripped of this easy revenue, it has become a matter of grave urgency for local newspapers to re-engage with their actual communities, as opposed to who they assume they can target commercially. Even prominent black newspaper journalists such as Hugh Muir on the *Guardian* stress that, although employment practices may have shifted a little, the underlying news values of journalism institutions remain those of middle-class white men (Francis, 2003), confirming that the textual prejudices exposed by media sociologist Teun Van Dijk (1993), which he called 'Elite Racism', still plague British journalism. Recent studies (Richardson, 2004; Greater London Authority, 2007; Runnymede, 2008) all highlight how representation within our news media still plays a part in the construction of a white society as the norm. Representation and news values continue to be shaped by the views and experiences of white upper-middle-class men despite attempts to engage with the employment of a more diverse clientele. Prominent black and Asian anchors on television mask the fact that journalists in Britain are still overwhelmingly white.

CLASS AND JOURNALISM EDUCATION

Social class also plays a large role in determining who will select a career in the news media and this has moved backwards if anything, despite universities' attempts to broaden access through their journalism courses. Delano and Henningham's (1995) groundbreaking report into the social composition of journalists conducted in the 1990s showed that nearly two-thirds of all new recruits described themselves as from middle-class backgrounds. The Journalism

Training Forum indicated that by 2003 less than 3 per cent of journalists come from families which were headed by parents from semi-skilled or unskilled backgrounds. The Sutton Trust's (2006) 'Educational Background of Leading Journalists' concludes in a similar fashion that they remain a largely white, middle-class breed. In addition, independent schools and Oxford and Cambridge university backgrounds provide a distinct advantage when it comes to the continuingly opaque route into the upper echelons of journalism in both broadcast and print. Another practice which is hostile to opening up journalism to more meritocratic patterns of recruitment is the growing prevalence of unpaid internships or work experience, which are now almost a prerequisite to gain the first toe-hold in an increasingly competitive industry. These are most likely to be affordable only to those whose parents have the financial resources to support their children and who can afford to locate these aspiring journalists in the extremely expensive London area where most of the news media placements are concentrated.

CONCLUSION

As in many other areas of Journalism Studies, education has been problematized by the complexity and contradictions inherent in the practice of journalism and the variety of employment within that practice. This has best been illustrated by empirical studies which have measured the changing nature and aspirations of the occupation and its historical efforts to engage with debates around professionalization.

The formal education of journalists, located predominantly as it is now in the HE sector, can assist in providing a form of journalism which is infused by the traditions of the public good and civic service, rather than allowing young new recruits to settle into a compromise with a jaded corporate cynicism which serves neither process nor product, audience nor practitioner. The university may have been slow out of the blocks in the provision of education but it is doing it seriously and effectively, having stepped in where previous attempts have proved half-hearted or lacking in sustained engagement. To a large extent this is a consequence of the increased institutional momentum emanating from the subject area as it has drawn to itself the best of both practical insight and interdisciplinary traditions of reflection and research.

In the current economic climate, there are, however, genuine concerns that the opportunities that may have sustained graduates through the traditional entry portals of journalism even a couple of years ago are no longer there. This is forcing a reconsideration of the breadth and nature of the curriculum as preparation for work in a much more fragmented and less secure working ecology. Both employers and students are likely to continue to demand that a degree in journalism provides a flexible and pragmatic engagement with a wider range of communicative practices than ever before. There is the additional anxiety that, as government funds are withdrawn from what are, in the main, expensive courses to teach, many of the more vocationally oriented new universities where journalism education has flourished may struggle to maintain provision at a rate which is affordable for its prospective students.

FURTHER READING

Allan (2005) has a chapter, 'Preparing reflective practitioners', in Keeble's *Print Journalism: An introduction*, Routledge, which gives an overview of developments in journalism training and education.

de Burgh (2005) *Making Journalists*, Routledge, is a thought-provoking edited collection of views on the current state of journalism training and education.

There are countless books on the market which take a student through the basics of skills and techniques, but the following are the pick of the bunch in this author's view in their ability to present the 'do's and don't's' without losing sight of the essential critical perspective. Each of the following provide highly reflective accounts of how to go about learning and teaching. Boyd (2008) *Broadcast Journalism: Techniques of television and radio news*, Focal Press; Beaman (2011) *Interviewing for Radio*, Routledge, now in its second edition; Keeble (2006) *The newspapers handbook*, Routledge, now in its fourth edition; de Burgh (2000) *Investigative Journalism*, Routledge. Hall (2001) *Online Journalism: A critical primer*, Pluto, was one of the first accounts of the challenges which digital technologies were throwing down for journalism practice and its audiences. Jones and Salter (2011) *Digital Journalism*, Sage, is an excellent up-to-the-minute account of the complexities and opportunities for both journalism and journalists within this emerging technological environment.

Gospill and Neale (2008) *Journalists: 100 years of the NUJ*, Profile, is a wide-ranging historical account of the contribution of the journalists' union to the formation of good practice, including ethical and educational standards.

Harcup (2007) *The Ethical Journalist*, Sage, is an exemplary combination of interviews with journalists and reflection on current ethical debate which can act as a lively and engaging introduction to a whole range of urgent issues which need to be considered by students entering upon studying the subject.

Holtz-Bacha and Frolich (eds) (2003) *Journalism Education in Europe and North America: An international comparison*, Hampton Press, gives a wide cross-section of approaches to the integration of journalism training within educational establishments.

Josephi (2010) *Journalism Education in Countries with Limited Media Freedom*, Peter Lang, draws on examples from China, Singapore, Cambodia, Oman, Egypt, Kenya, Brazil, Russia and Romania to explore an often neglected aspect of journalism education.

3

JOURNALISM STUDIES AND RESEARCH APPROACHES

INTRODUCTION

Journalism Studies is defined as much as an area of research as a subject to be taught. At most universities you will be taught within an environment which insists that all teaching is informed by research and scholarship. This is true of subjects across the board. The best universities have staff who are actively engaged in shaping the field through their own research and their modules will mesh with and enrich the practical instruction. Less research-intensive universities will still provide course content which draws upon this research as part of the scholarly environment. Research into Journalism Studies is a vital part of the subject being taken seriously by universities and provides an essential intellectual framework.

This chapter will explore how this research has evolved, what its disciplinary traditions are and will stake a claim for its importance to contemporary journalism beyond the academy. As an area for research, Journalism Studies is located between the social sciences and the humanities. The inevitable complexity of this location is amplified by the variety of perspectives which are brought to bear upon it. It must consider the experience of those practising journalism where relevant, that of former practitioners who are now working as educators and researchers, the consumers of journalism – its audience – other disciplinary fields which research the products of journalism, as well as its own developing academic identity. The need for an area of scholarship to embrace contemporary professional practice is not unique. Education, law and medicine are good examples of this. Yet these fields of knowledge have longer professional and academic traditions, while journalism, as we saw in the previous chapter, continues to have conflicting issues around its own professionalism. Approaches to research in Journalism Studies have emerged at differing speeds and differing rates of maturity and from directions within the academy. These vary from Mass Communications to Linguistics and from English Literature to Psychology. Perhaps it is as a consequence of this complexity, the accumulated weight and the wealth of these areas of research, that something often considered outside the scope of serious study should have evolved so rapidly as a research area in its own right.

MULTIDISCIPLINARITY

It is therefore fair to say that Journalism Studies is a multi-disciplinary field of research. Multidisciplinarity is not only an accurate reflection of the variety of inputs to the field, it is also important in bringing an appreciation that no one approach or sectional appeal can be adequate to a full appraisal of journalism's impact or importance. For instance, political economic, historical, ethnographic or social science approaches all have validity but none can claim primacy, given that the very nature of journalism means that it is doing a complex variety of things, sometimes simulta-neously and often changing in particular geographical and historical contexts. For example, a report on the royal wedding of 2011 has political importance; historical resonance; serious celebrity gossip potential; is an important indicator of an aspect of British tradition within a changing global environment; can be used to increase sales at home; is a visual extravaganza for photographers; is a columnist's dream as each vies with rivals for an individual take on the event; is an important aspect of the newspaper's editorial identity. I could go on! All of these aspects can provide studies within the con-temporary research community, analysed from different national perspectives or traded upon historically in times to come. The growing acknowledgement of the sort of systematic scrutiny which research activity brings is a great complement to contemporary journalism. Here we will explore the strands of research which have combined into such a vibrant area of engagement.

ROOTS OF A RESEARCH TRADITION

Just as journalism education emerged within the institutional traditions available to it in the UK, research into journalism as an academic area in its own right has developed by borrowing research approaches from cognate areas such as sociology, mass communications, applied linguistics, ethnography, history and political studies, to name only the most productive. In Britain some of the earliest academic work emanated from a tradition which became identified as 'cultural studies', which had its roots in the sort of political and linguistic critique of the press which Orwell had pioneered in the left-wing *Tribune* magazine in the early 1940s. The post-war adult education environment encouraged investigations of class, education and literacy, notably in the work of Raymond Williams and Richard Hoggart. In *The Long Revolution* Williams (1961) explored the complex genesis of the English popular press, and later in *Television: Technology and Cultural Form* (Williams, 1974) he argued for a cultural perspective on the ways in which television had become incorporated into the way people organized their daily lives, opposing views of this technological innovation which suggested people were almost the victims of technology. Earlier, Richard Hoggart's (1957) *The Uses of Literacy* railed polemically against what he considered the depoliticization of the post-war English working classes by considering the impact of mass media including magazines and the popular newspaper, which he saw as 'unbending the springs of action'.

FROM DESCRIPTION TO ANALYSIS: FRANKFURT TO BIRMINGHAM

Journalism has long been considered, from certain perspectives, as a form of social control rather than the means of political emancipation espoused by some of its more optimistic advocates. Serious consideration of the possible role of journalism as an agent of control emerged indirectly following the tradition of research from the Frankfurt School from the 1930s (e.g. Horkheimer, Adorno), who had witnessed the rise of Hitler and were understandably disturbed about the potential impact of mass media on what were often asserted to be passive audiences. Their work in exile developed into a full-blown and negative critique of the influence of mass media in the United States in the 1940s and 1950s. Early experiments with political readings of the news media in Britain were consolidated when Hoggart established an institutional home for this work from 1964 at the University of Birmingham's Centre for Contemporary Cultural Studies. It was from this centre that we begin to see a more sustained critique from the late 1960s onwards, one which moves beyond descriptive assessments to more systematic analysis. As important as the critique was in itself, the institutional setting was even more important, as it allowed a gathering of like-minded scholars to generate an intellectual climate of enquiry. The centre brought much-needed scrutiny of news media practices which had previously been considered as either neutral or natural. Stuart Hall took over the director's role in 1968 and began a long series of political interventions which would prompt new ways of asking questions about the broader social and political role of journalism. The 1973 paper entitled 'Encoding/decoding' became a classic statement of the Birmingham Centre's approach to the cultural and political production of news and how it considered that news positions its audiences through its routines of selection and presentation. It was influential in establishing an extremely productive model for the exploration of political and cultural power. Hall and his colleagues at Birmingham were politically motivated in that they insisted upon the ideological positioning of the news media, in part through their use of language, as representatives of institutionalized power structures. The analysis of the word 'mugging' to demonstrate how it was being used systematically to racialize street crime in London was a particularly powerful moment for the research. Reading news reports critically and against the grain of the news media's own intentions was an act of resistance for these most politically engaged of scholars. Work closely related in its approach included Cohen and Young's (1973) *The Manufacture of News*, which, as the title suggests, provided an account of journalism as a construction of reality which depended upon long-term patterns to develop its consensual political viewpoints on what was politically and culturally acceptable, especially in terms of crime and morality. The combination of these sorts of critical approach laid the foundation for later work from other centres which derived from a sociological perspective, such as Chibnall (1977) and Schlesinger and Tumber's (1995) *Reporting Crime*.

Work from this direction is still prominent, including the most recent example from one of the original researchers at the centre, Critcher (2003), whose book on moral panics did much to focus attention once again on the role of the news media in setting and indeed sometimes skewing national political and social agendas.

GLASGOW ENTERS THE FRAY

The disciplinary home for much of the research emerging within this British tradition was in the sociology departments which began to be established from the 1960s. Here the role of the journalist and journalism in constructing and amplifying the world became a key concern. The work of the Frankfurt School was reprinted in anthologies on media criticism in the UK from the 1970s and had a significant impact on perceptions of journalism as a potential area for political activity and critical engagement. The Glasgow Media Group (1976) provided the most sustained of the university research approaches in the 1970s. Its participants focused attention on the lack of coverage of the perspective of the trade unions or the workers they represented within news media reports of industrial disputes. There was a hostile reception from within many sections of the news media industries towards the content analyses of the Glasgow Media Group. A notable response to their methods was published by Harrison (1985), *Television News: Whose Bias?*, which was in fact funded by one of the news companies critiqued, Independent Television News! Criticisms from within the news media industries such as this emphasized that they had produced work which may not have adequately reflected the pressures which journalists were under during the processes of news gathering and production. The news media in their defence argued that this academic critique may not have been as aware as it might have been of the professional traditions and institutional constraints within which journalism was produced. Yet it would be unfair to single these scholars out as having generated the only negative view of the political implications of much journalism. There was already a strong tradition of scepticism regarding journalism in the elite tradition of high cultural suspicion which one can trace through from the Victorian period to F.R. Leavis and others in the 1920s and 1930s. The academic studies of the 1950s to the 1970s at least went out of their way to provide samples and analysis rather than the sort of cultural knee-jerk of the earlier culturalists. Such sustained research scrutiny at least served to put television journalism on its mettle. It was being taken seriously as a communication form with real social and political impact and needed to begin responding to informed observations from critical participants who had hitherto often being silent about that communication process.

Another benefit of critics such as the Glasgow Media Group was that they provided a timely corrective to professional protestations of balance as a professional code. It is still producing highly provocative and productive work to this day. Winston (2002), for example, has revisited the GMG's earliest claims and provides a persuasive account which justifies its positions, claiming that they did a lot to jolt journalism into a recognition of the fundamentally political nature of much of what it had previously assumed was governed by traditions of professional responsibility and common sense.

SEMIOLOGY AND CULTURAL STUDIES

From a different cultural perspective and a different critical tradition the collection of essays, *Mythologies*, Roland Barthes's popularization of the work of Swiss linguist Ferdinand de Saussure, lit the fuse of critical linguistic study. It became a foundational text for British cultural criticism. First published in France in 1957, it was only after its translation as late as 1973 that it began to be used to structure criticism of media forms in the English-speaking world. It triggered the production of several influential books which sought to apply semiotic insights into the products of television and print news. Fiske and Hartley's (1978) *Reading Television* and Hartley's (1982) *Understanding News* both applied the insights of semiology to the forms of written and visual journalism through the prism of Barthes's work.

Semiology and social critique combined with emerging traditions in philosophy and English literature to form a new wave of Critical

Theory which was to shape many studies of journalism in the 1980s. The field which became categorized as British Cultural Studies was to a large extent responsible for drawing attention to the products of British culture such as newspapers, television news and film as sources for analytical work. British Cultural Studies provided an extremely varied set of readings of popular contemporary culture through the lenses of post-structuralism, literary theory, Marxist theory, feminism and semiology. More often than not, it continued to read journalism against the accounts of many of its practitioners, viewing journalism not as a conduit for information but as a form of cultural production in its own right. It implied a very sceptical view of any claim that journalism is merely dealing in facts and challenged journalism's claims to objective procedural traditions at the same time as it forced a reconsideration of the narratives that journalism had told about itself. This critique was analytically more complex but less directly political than that of the 1960s and 1970s. These traditions laid the foundations for the critical discussion of journalism as it began its sustained entry into the university sector from the early 1990s. As the area of Journalism Studies has matured, it has begun to engage more fully with a selection of research methods combined and moulded very much to its own specific needs. Some of these are discussed briefly below.

JOURNALISM LAW

Theory and practice are woven by necessity throughout an increasing number of areas of journalism. This is nowhere more evident than in the case of media law as it applies to journalists. Journalists are expected to be truthful and to adhere to the laws of the land in gaining access to information and in publishing it. Journalism law is first and foremost a means for journalists, if not staying out of the courts where they need to be to report on proceedings, then at least out of the dock. It is based on the examples of past practice known as Case Law and by definition this needs to be constantly considered and taught afresh to each generation of students. There are books written which set out to guide students and current professionals through the maze of the legal constraints on journalism, such as McNae's – the most recent versions authored by Hanna and Banks (2009), now in its twentieth edition – and

Quinn's (2011) *Law for Journalists*, first published in 2007 and now in its second edition. Such books are written by former and current journalists and lawyers who have responsibility for the delivery of law courses at universities where part of their function is to reflect upon and contribute to discussions of media law in general through their research. There are other books, such as Rozenberg's (2004) *Privacy and the Press*, where journalists specializing in the area of the law contribute their expertise to the ongoing debate.

In practical terms, it pays for journalists and aspiring journalists to engage with discussions of legislation on the shifting parameters of privacy law, contempt of court and libel, for example. In fact, no editor would want someone working for them who did not have an up-to-date knowledge of the legal aspects of journalism. Libel can be an expensive business. Journalism law must be taught and examined for editors to be confident in the abilities of graduates to be able to handle the basics of the job. The NCTJ sets law exams for students and novices to journalism. At best, this is taught within an environment informed by research into the latest considerations of the substance of journalism and its engagement with the shifting sands of legal requirements together with social awareness of the broader implications of such legislation. Such extended reflection of how the law combines with institutional expectations has become a critical point at the BBC in the wake of the Hutton Report. No law had been broken when Gilligan reported a version of events which was deemed to have departed from the BBC's expectations of accuracy but the Corporation felt it had let down its public and itself in allowing opinion to ride too prominently to the fore in a story.

It is research-led work which is currently exploring the new challenges to traditional legal frameworks posed by online sourcing, the potential of the internet to circumvent 'super-injunctions', the status of bloggers and their liability for libel and the desirability for journalists to maintain a distance from the chatter of the online population. A distinct contribution to this comes in the work of the Centre for Law, Justice and Journalism at City University, led by Lorna Woods. This draws together expertise in journalism, law and criminology to provide a range of research driven by a consideration of the state of journalism from the perspective of its legal requirements.

JOURNALISM ETHICS

Related to these strictly legal frameworks, there are also ethical conventions which need to keep pace with public sensitivities and the changing social demands on journalism. There is a direct linkage between the behaviour of journalists, the credibility of their practice and the economic sustainability of journalism as articulated by Raymond Snoddy in a study which emanated from the crisis in journalism, which led to the Calcutt Committee's Report (1990) and its disbanding of the Press Council and setting up of the Press Complaints Commission in 1991. It was a sustained critique of the practices of popular journalism from within an industry which had come to suspect that it was impossible to offend public taste. Building upon a similar analysis from Tom Baistow (1985) almost a decade previously indicating how little had changed in the meantime, Snoddy's perspective was undoubtedly sharpened by his role as media correspondent at that time for the *Financial Times*. He knew that legislation to control all newspapers was just around the corner if the press could not restrain its urge for the lurid and the intrusive. It is worth quoting his conclusions in full:

> In the end, talking about and encouraging high standards and ethics in newspapers – tabloids as well as broadsheets – is not some sort of self-indulgence for amateur moral philosophers or journalists with sensitive psyches: it is a very practical matter, involving customer relations, product improvement and profit ... Unless such issues are taken more seriously, future generations could be reading about many of today's newspapers in the history books, rather than actually reading the papers themselves.
>
> (Snoddy, 1993: 203)

Interestingly enough, it was not media scholars but Belsey and Chadwick (1992), as philosophers, who were the first to provide a popular and wide-ranging edited collection of discussions on ethical issues in journalism, albeit from within a university school at Cardiff, which at that point encompassed both philosophy and journalism. This is eloquent testimony to the benefits of interdisciplinary discussions of journalism within a research environment and one which went some way to facilitating developments in ethics modules for journalism students. Sometimes journalism needs a little help from its neighbours! Research on journalism ethics has blossomed ever since and this has to a large degree been prompted by the need for its ethical aspects to be taught within the broader expectations of university education. The growth of university courses has had the benefit of encouraging an elaboration of journalism ethics beyond the Codes of Conduct and the varied manuals of house style. Journalists-turned-educators such as Chris Frost (2000), Richard Keeble (2001) – both now in second editions – and Tony Harcup (2006) have all produced guides which set out an approach which is idealistically ambitious yet which still offers practical guidance in maintaining ethical standards in the pursuit of information. The approaches to ethics within this research agenda range from the discussion of general conventions to deliberations on political and moral responsibilities. In much of this published work there is clear evidence that the requirements of teaching journalism at university level have led to a gestation of critical views on the ethics of journalism beyond a simple pragmatism of what you can get away with without being actually prosecuted or sacked. In general terms, this research has been good for journalism education and its standing within the university, even if it continues to struggle to make itself felt within journalism practice.

REGULATION AND REFLECTION

In addition to hard legal requirements there are the more subtle regulatory pressures of codes of conduct from the Press Complaints Commission, the National Union of Journalists and the BBC Producers' Guidelines. These are in turn scrutinized and assessed as to their efficacy by researchers and academics on behalf of both industry and the wider critical community. In this case we have an example of research acting as an effective voice of the watchdogs of the watchdogs! Frost (2004), for instance, has provided the best piece of recent research on the facts and figures of the first ten years of the Press Complaints Commission, which demonstrates that it has proved to be a less than impressive operation, surveying the evidence to support criticisms that it lacks teeth, is too weighted in favour of the press's vested interests and investigates too few cases brought to its attention.

The regulation of journalism has long been a topic for sustained investigation. Political debate on the content and management of public service broadcasting, for example, has been a hot potato since the Sykes Committee set out its principles in 1923. Regulation issues are often accompanied by a reasonably public debate, as in the case of campaigning organizations such as Presswise 1993 (Mediawise from 2005) or the Campaign for Press and Broadcasting Freedom, founded in 1979. Increasingly, academics are following in the tradition established by the Royal Commissions on the Press (1949, 1962, 1977) by being invited by politicians to contribute expert opinion to debates on news media matters for the House of Lords Communications Committee and on assessments of the Calcutt Inquiry (Bingham, 2007), the effectiveness of Ofcom (Petley, 2006; 2008) or unsolicited but influential assessments such as Frost's mentioned above. The research publications of these academics is the reason they are invited to contribute to debate, demonstrating the linkage between academic research in the area and their public reputation beyond their own university.

Journalists are not licensed professionals, so cannot be struck off any list of approved practitioners, but they can be imprisoned or fired even if they later return to write another day for a different organization. Andrew Gilligan, sacked by the BBC for his part in the report on 29 May 2003 which led indirectly to the death of weapons inspector David Kelly, was soon in full employment once again, while the resignation of the *News of the World* editor Andy Coulson, after his Royal Correspondent had been jailed for hacking into the mobile phones of various celebrities, was followed by his appointment as Director of Communications for David Cameron's Conservative Party.

JOURNALISM HISTORY

There have been formal histories of journalism from the mid-nineteenth century onwards. The first was Andrews (1847), and this was followed by Bourne (1887). These were stirring attempts to provide an overview of the importance of the contribution of journalism to longer processes of political enlightenment and did not shy away from demonstrating how journalism had often depended on the work of political and social outsiders and how it had not always been as altruistic as some retrospective personal accounts might have been tempted to suggest. They served as an antidote to a more substantial set of contributions, the biographies and even autobiographies which were more often than not related from the perspective of the great and the good – most often the owners and editors of newspapers.

The journalism of the nineteenth century has been privileged in research terms because of its proximity to the research interests of scholars of literature and the Victorian era's importance for long-itudinal studies of a range of cultural and social issues (Brown, 1985; Jones, 1996; Wiener, 1988). Much contemporary research into journalism flows from this relatively early crossover. This has flourished recently in the quite magnificent *Dictionary of Nineteenth Century Journalism* (Brake and Demoor, 2009), which provides an absolutely essential reference text for any exploration of journalism's nineteenth-century contexts.

Despite this tradition, an account of journalism which was detached from genuine historical enquiry and from the uses which history was making of the texts of journalism was manifest through much of the twentieth century, notably with contributions such as Symon's (1914) *The Press and Its Story*, Harold Herd's (1953) *The March of Journalism* and Stanley Morison's (1932) *The English Newspaper*. All of these, in varying ways, reduced journalism's wide cultural impact to a narrative concentrating on the achievements of important individual editors and the personified energies of indivi-dual newspapers. Even better-researched histories such as Siebert's (1965) account of the rise and fall of government control of the press in England over three centuries still managed to represent the press as the ultimate victor in a struggle for independence from government, as if the restrictions and control of owners, advertisers and markets played little or no part in structuring the survival and economic success of newspapers. Koss's account, which, though compendious, similarly restricts the role of the press to a rather narrow vehicle for political communication while ignoring its broader cultural engagement as well as anything outside the most politically oriented newspapers. Journalism history for too long in research terms has been naïve history.

Frank's (1961) detailed analysis of the language and structure of the birth of English journalism during the English Civil War

(1642–51) is an exceptional demonstration of what could be achieved with a more precise and culturally attuned agenda. Historians started to signal an interest in journalism as something other than a background for their own work, possibly with Cranfield's work on both local and national press from 1962. Boyce, Curran and Wingate (1978) pioneered one of the first compilations from a broad range of scholars from communications backgrounds, highlighting 'the way in which the role of the press is perceived, the expectations of audiences, the values and beliefs of newspapermen, the attitudes of elites to the press [as] all significant in helping us to understand the nature and development [of journalism]'. One of the editors of the book, James Curran, provided a hugely influential counter-narrative to the likes of Siebert and Koss, arguing that the commercial emancipation of the press from overt political control in Britain from 1855 had provided a smokescreen for the more effective economic control of political opinion in the press and that this had formed part of a new, more subtle and arguably more effective form of social control: the control of the market. Curran later joined forces with Jean Seaton to produced a highly successful account of the development of British journalism (Curran and Seaton, 1981). It was celebrated for the way it located contemporary issues within a critical historical framework, which privileged a political account of how markets had shaped the course of journalism, often to the detriment of accountability and diversity. Seaton's account of the BBC was of an organization constantly attempting to resist both political pressure and commercial pressure from damaging its own limited attempts to fashion a public service alternative to commercially driven journalism. Despite this, broadcast journalism has not generated as much in terms of sustained historical study as the press. It has seen some excellent work on the archives of broadcasting institutions and some outstanding institutional histories, but the nature of much of the output which needs studying makes it more difficult to return to than print archives, which have the advantage of access as they are often stored in more than one location and are increasingly available online. Among the work on broadcasting, Briggs's (1961, 1965, 1970a, 1970b, 1995) multiple-volume history of the BBC sets an extraordinarily high standard, but its very reach prevents it from engaging as fully as it might with what is in effect merely part of the BBC's output, its journalism.

Smith (1973) provided an insightful account of the implications of radio technology, particularly for journalism, and this was supplemented by Williams's (1974) equally provocative account of the cultural implications of television technology. For a long time Crisell's (1994) account of radio and television journalism was a lone overview but this has been complemented more recently by Street's (2002) more specific account of the history of radio journalism and Crisell's (1997) own more specific exploration of radio journalism's development. One of the forerunners of social accounts of broadcasting's influence was the fascinating but sadly incomplete interpretation of the social implications of radio journalism covered by the work of Scannell and Cardiff (1991). Scannell (1996) returned some years later to the philosophical implications of broadcast journalism and this has dovetailed with work on the archives of the BBC produced by Nicholas and the polemic accounts of O'Malley (1994, 2001) on the demise of the BBC's public service capability.

Hendy's (2007) impressive contemporary work on BBC Radio Four is equally authoritative and complete in its engagement with the specifically journalistic output of one of the BBC's channels. Blumler and Franklin (1990) had already produced the report on the experimental introduction of the televising of Parliament and, later, this tradition was complemented by Franklin's (2005) editing of the MacTaggart lecture series on television policy at the Edinburgh Festival, which provided a significant moment in the development of public studies of public service journalism. This edited collection was the first opportunity to reflect on the totality of these presentations within the scholarly context earlier provided by Franklin himself (Franklin, 2001). Recent additions to a new series published by Sage, Journalism Studies: Key Texts, give additional historical perspective to the generic/technological range of journalism which the series covers, including magazines, radio, television, newspapers and online journalism.

THE RECEPTION OF HISTORY

The benefit of sustained historical research seems obvious as it sheds light in the long run on our understanding of journalism's concrete contribution to the broadest possible conceptions of political and social life. In addition, historical research can help to relativize the 'golden age' which had been proclaimed as the heyday of journalism in the nineteenth century (Ensor, 1968) and shift focus away from the self-justifying narratives of the retired 'great and good'. Former journalist turned media commentator and Professor of Journalism at City University, Roy Greenslade, comments on the new generation of histories (2005: 74–5) that, of all the myths spread by journalists, none is as enduring as the story about a past golden age and that one of the benefits of the revisionist histories provided by historians working within Journalism Studies is that they debunk these myths. He claims that reading such accounts would benefit practising journalists too. Too narrow a historical engagement plays into the hands of the surfeit of insider accounts which, although interesting on their own terms, fail to relate journalism's history to any of its overlapping relationships within broader social, political and cultural trends. This has tended to impoverish the history of journalism until relatively recently. Joad Raymond, writing from within the more established tradition of English Literature, has done much to reinvigorate the work of Frank in exploring the specific characteristics of Civil War news culture both by himself and in collaboration with scholars in an impressive edited collection (Raymond, 1996, 1999).

The issues facing historical journalism research are now articulated as a part of a growing international and multidisciplinary field with a great deal of sophistication and a measure of maturity. The paradoxes and problems of such study are being considered by Curran (2002, 2009) and Bailey (2009), among others, doing in effect for British journalism history studies what Schudson, Carey, Barnhurst and Nerone have done for the US version. Outside Britain and the USA, journalism history is a growing part of debates in Australia, Southern Africa, Western Europe, China and Latin America with special issues of journals, research centres and international conferences demonstrating its appeal as Journalism Studies research develops worldwide.

OBSERVATIONAL STUDIES

Observational studies have provided an essential strategy to help allay suspicions that all research into journalism concentrates merely on the texts, the products of the news media, without due consideration of the processes which the journalists had to work within in order to produce their work. Textual studies are worthy in themselves but limited as all research methods are in isolation. In their favour, observational studies can bring a methodological approach to enhance broader understandings of the working world of the journalist. Schlesinger (1978) and Golding and Elliott's (1979) early work highlighted the routinization of news production for both radio and television and also the social and managerial hierarchies at work in public service broadcast journalism. Criticisms were made by the institutions studied that they did not emphasize the space for autonomy for journalists within these systems. Subsequently, Machin and Niblock (2006) and Harrison (2006) have further refined these models and deployed research on the ethnography of the newsroom into explorations of how journalists have incorporated recent technological developments into their daily routines.

POPULAR CULTURE

For too long popular journalism had been considered of no value at all for the purposes of prolonged study unless it were as an example of how journalism could be used to whip up populist prejudices. There was certainly part of the tradition emanating from Hoggart and the Birmingham Centre which held popular journalism in very low regard. Pieces of early work which disputed what had become the dominant account were Fiske's (1987, 1989) championing of the resistant power of popular readers in determining the value of popular texts for themselves. This acted as a productive counterposition to what had become an unambiguous torrent of criticism of popular journalism from both left and right. An international research seminar in Dubrovnik in 1990 prompted a concentration on what had hitherto been a neglected area of journalism research, despite the fact that popular journalism had long provided the bulk of the journalism consumed in Britain. Dahlgren and Sparks provided the forum for what would be a highly influential set of debates on the importance of journalism's role in popular culture more generally with their publication of the papers from this seminar in 1992.

Before this, there had been an excellent if rather low-profile study of the significance of the page 3 girl in the *Sun* by Patricia Holland in 1984, intriguingly entitled 'The page 3 girl speaks to women too', which was keen to provide an explanation of the appeal of heterosexual pleasure to a new generation of working-class readers, addressed as consumers. However, in the main, most studies had continued to draw more or less explicitly on earlier work by Williams, Hoggart and Hall. The break which began with Fiske preferred to take a more nuanced, culturalist account of how this form of journalism meshed with the range of everyday pleasures of ordinary people while downplaying the explicitly politicized nature of some of the earlier critiques. Journalism was presented as a constituent of popular culture not as something separate from it. Such an approach drew in a wide range of sympathetic critics, keen to address the hitherto neglected role of the popular. Engel (1996) tackled the twentieth-century popular press and his book is notable for being both a serious historical account from a popular perspective as well as being written by a practising journalist – although not one writing on a popular newspaper, taking a sabbatical from the *Guardian* as he was at the time. Hartley (1996), in the same year, provided an iconoclastic reading of popular journalism as popular reality. Rubery's (2009) later study of the role of sensationalism in nineteenth-century popular journalism is a good illustration of how approaches within traditional historical research are now engaging with the specific appeal of popular print journalism. Bingham (2004, 2009) explores the gendered nature of much of popular journalism's output across the twentieth century and Conboy (2002, 2006) has provided a longitudinal assessment of the specifics of popular journalism's appeal as well as a contemporary snapshot of the linguistics of the tabloid press. Nadoo's (2009) recent contribution to the series Science, Technology and Medicine in Modern History draws extensively on news media sources to illustrate how popular representations of science are constructed, in her case the heart transplants of the 1960s.

LINGUISTIC APPROACHES

A nineteenth-century comic dialogic begins:

'What, Garniston? Corrupting your style by studying a newspaper!'

For a long time, the language of journalism was not considered a worthy subject of study at all. It was trapped within assumptions that what was produced quickly was produced without much in the way of thoughtfulness and was consequently of little use in analysing social or cultural trends. Journalism was taken, perhaps too literally, at its own word, as a medium whose main task was to convey the news of the day as quickly and effectively as possible. A notable historian of the press has recalled the fact that it was referred to as 'fugitive literature' (Jones, 1996) for this very reason. There were aspects of journalistic output in magazine and review form which might have had pretensions to greater literary merit but the general fare of the press was considered sub-literary, or even sub-literate, by elite cultural producers if not by its paying customers. Research has enabled the language of journalism to be recuperated as an area of serious and relevant study.

Things began to change in the 1950s, when a revival of interest in a hitherto obscure Swiss linguist called Ferdinand de Saussure indicated that language could be used as an avenue for more general social exploration as part of an expanding interest in the study of culture and anthropology. This was to prove especially relevant for areas such as the language and imagery of popular culture, particularly journalism, which had been largely ignored by serious academic researchers. The first study to incorporate this sort of analysis into a specific consideration of newspaper language was Smith's (1975) *Paper Voices*. This charted the rise of the two most popular newspapers of their era, the *Daily Express* and the *Daily Mirror*, by exploring how they used language to amplify their appeal to specific readerships. Interestingly, Smith's book has a foreword from Stuart Hall, who was to gain his reputation in a series of parallel investigations of the politics and sociology of the news. The Glasgow Media Group from 1976 also drew very heavily on insights provided by sociolinguistics in their research on the framing as well as the content of broadcast news in particular.

Building on the momentum of these rather isolated studies with newspaper language at their heart, in the late 1970s a group of academics from the University of East Anglia began the sort of systematic engagement with the language of the press which would become known as discourse analysis. Hodge, Kress, Fowler and Trew, in 1979, started to look at the patterning of language choices in the news media, revealing what a casual first reading did not. What they were interested in was the patterning across news stories of assumptions and implicit meanings which can add up to a subtle, undeclared political worldview, often referred to in the literature as ideology, which is out of sight of the immediacy of the news production environment but worthy of comment and analysis nevertheless. This is another ideological engagement with journalism which ultimately leads to a more sensitized linguistic environment and to the possibility of greater awareness of the rhetorical range of the news media among readers. Hodge and Kress (1979) are most explicit in *Language as Ideology* and both they and Fowler (1991) in *Language in the News* have the education of media consumers very much to the fore in their research. Building on the work emerging from East Anglia's English Department, Searle's (1989) *Your Daily Dose: Racism in the Sun* was an impassioned demonstration of how the patterning of news concerning black Britain is unequivocally offensive and demeaning when it is collected and analysed. This polemic contribution to academic debate acted as a cold shower to the self-esteem of liberal journalists, as it demonstrated that racism in the press was not simply a matter of individual racist intent, but more a product of the practices of sensationalism and simplification often foregrounded in the language of news media. The realization of the impact that such ignorance can have on the lives of black Britons and the impression on the white majority forced journalists, especially at the popular end of the market, to reconsider claims that their reports were merely telling the story. The language of journalism is much more influential than that.

Such studies became consolidated in what became known as Critical Discourse Analysis with research from Fowler, Fairclough, van Dijk and Wodak and the founding in 1990 of the interdisciplinary journal *Discourse and Society*. This publication was an important institutional moment and, although its scope is considerably broader than the language of the news, it nevertheless provided a focal point for sustained topical study of these issues. Critical Discourse Analysis asserts that inequality is expressed through the patterns of representation to be found in news media texts in general rather than in isolated examples and that these patterns are often established within the traditions and styles which have become established as normal within particular newspapers.

Richardson (2004) has provided interesting complementary work on the contemporary coverage of Muslims in the British press. It is noteworthy particularly because of its concentration on the elite rather than the popular press, demonstrating the tenuousness of claims that liberal journalism's representation of ethnic 'outsiders' is less prejudicial than that of the popular tabloids.

The particular approach termed conversational analysis was used by Heritage under van Dijk's editorial tutelage in 1985 and this was deployed in Greatbatch's (1988) work, which explored the news interview in Britain. In 1991 Scannell provided an impressive range of insightful research into broadcast language, work which was complemented recently by Montgomery's (2007) reflections on language in this medium. Montgomery's fastidious work opens the way for systematic studies of the wide range of radio journalism's language which, because it is much more time-consuming to analyse, fleeting as it is in comparison with print-based texts, has always suffered in comparison with critical analysis of the language of newspapers.

Further investigations probed the hitherto cosy assertions of the internal logic of house styles, with Deborah Cameron (1996) claiming that when scrutinized it was clear that protestations that they were simply exercises in efficiency or clarity or commonsense tradition did not stand up to any sustained examination, which in fact revealed them as deeply connected to the dominant ideas within the newspaper or news media brand and therefore irretrievably ideological in impact if not in intent.

Golding, Billig and colleagues from the Department of Sociology at the University of Loughborough demonstrated something of the crossover appeal of this sort of linguistic analysis in their coverage of political campaigns. They were routinely hired by elite national newspapers to provide quantifiable research on the language of election campaigns in the 1990s and 2000s. This provided a full circle of impact in its reflection on the language of political representation in the media themselves! A key moment in this sort of research into the language of politics was Fairclough's (2000) brief and highly accessible account of the New Labour project as a primarily linguistic enterprise, including its targeting of their cultivation of image in the national press.

Journalism has provided a fertile area of interdisciplinary research between history and linguistics. The deployment of Corpus

Linguistics developed at the University of Zurich in approaches to journalism history, combined with the relatively early digitization of Early English Books Online, has meant that we have moved swiftly from an economy of scarcity of resources to one of plenty and even overabundance. Early computer-enhanced research enabled seven-teenth- and eighteenth-century material to be studied with greater ease and efficiency than ever before. The *Journal of Historical Pragmatics*, established in 2000, has been key to developments in this field. Now as nineteenth- and twentieth-century material is added to these collections in the large-scale digitizations of both public and private newspaper and magazine collections, the promise for more effective longitudinal studies is even greater.

LITERARY JOURNALISM

There has been a long-established interest in the journalistic output of several star journalists down the centuries, Defoe, Addison and Steele, Swift, Johnson, Dickens, to name only the most prominent. Such research was often driven by interest from within literary studies and it explored their language in the tradition of literary criticism. More recently there has been a renewed interest in the generic and stylistic features of journalism on its own terms. This has seen the development of a journal, *the Journal of Literary Journalism*, dedicated to literary journalism since 2009 via the International Association for Literary Journalism Studies, which was itself founded in 2006 and which organizes a regular conference and publications ranging from debates on the merits of a range of foreign correspondents and the work of a range of idiosyncratic columnists to the journalistic output of authors who are often better known for their novels. Inglis (2002) had worked on this interest to provide an overview of war correspondents' style. An interesting feature of this literary emphasis in general is that women who have traditionally been marginalized in historical accounts of the range of journalistic style are more prominently featured in such studies. Such explorations help us to appreciate the aspects of style which make journalism distinct at the same time as encouraging us to consider the fullest range of literary output which has a journalistic component to it. Angela Phillips has contributed to the stylistic analysis of what makes good writing for journalism in similar fashion, with a book published in 2007. She draws on significant experience, having worked across genres and styles of publications from early feminist periodical *Spare Rib* to regular features in the *Guardian* in a career spanning over thirty years.

POLITICAL ECONOMY

The most basic understanding of journalism is that, when stripped of all its ideals and democratic aspirations, it needs to make a profit. However, this has more often than not been shelved in more elevated discussions of journalism's political or cultural impact or taken for granted to such an extent that it has not been considered worthy of serious analysis. And yet the profit-making imperative has huge implications for the structure, content and audiences of journalism. By the 1960s, on the back of work exploring the political content of the news media, the approach which became known as political economy took stock of the implications of ownership and institutional structure for the products of journalism. Explorations of the workings of advanced capitalism had developed to the point that the news media now also fell under this analytical gaze. It became most fully incorporated within studies of journalism in the work by Garnham (1979). Curran et al. (1980) explored the ways that human interest stories proved commercially attractive at the same time as they systematically marginalized other types of news, including political reporting. American scholars Herman and Chomsky (1988) provided a searing analysis of the political and economic motivations of much mainstream journalism and the implicit and explicit structures of censorship and gatekeeping which these give rise to. Their account has provided a highly transferable and still highly relevant approach for students of the news media today. Golding and Murdock (1991) combined, not for the first time, to produce an in-depth account of the confluence of culture, communications and political economy. This approach has developed a sophistication which could account for the actions of relatively autonomous and politically critical participants at the same time as highlighting the structural constraints which are expressed in professional norms and duties. Cottle (2003) and Doyle (2003) have provided the most recent interpretations of the political economy model which explore the complexities at work in the contemporary world where journalism operates as one aspect of global conglomerate communication industries.

Of particular contemporary interest is one piece of work emanating from the Reuters Institute for the Study of Journalism at Oxford University. The title of this collection of essays edited by Levy and Nielsen (2010) is expressive of its dominant theme: *The Changing Business of Journalism and Its Implications for Democracy*. The book addresses the central issue of its title in a range of countries and finds much common concern about how technological innovations are being embraced in ways that on the one hand appear to threaten traditional models of news media engagement with politics but on the other offer an opportunity for journalism to commit to a renewal of many of its core principles. One of the key aspects of the book is that it draws upon empirical and other authoritative sources to challenge any view of technology as sweeping all before it. It is a call for journalists as well as policy makers to reconsider the political economy of the news media for new times.

POLITICAL COMMUNICATION

For all that journalism had claimed for centuries that it was a vital component of the democratic process, there was very little sustained research into how the two interacted until late in the twentieth century. This is particularly puzzling given that, unlike in France and the United States, where there was a demonstrable evidence of print culture formally impacting upon political reality in their respective revolutionary traditions, the situation in Britain was characterized by a set of laissez-faire assertions which idealized a great deal of the role of journalism but which could demonstrate very little in tangible terms other than having persisted and ground the opposition down. It was hardly auspicious evidence for serious investigation of journalism's proud boasts to be acting as a watchdog operating on behalf of the public.

Journalism's own account of its traditions as characterized as a Fourth Estate are particularly relevant here. Macauley (1828) had referred to the journalists sitting in Parliament as a Fourth Estate of the realm, adding their weight and scrutiny of the political process to the other three traditional estates (the House of Commons, the House of Lords and the Church), but Carlyle claimed that the term had been used before this in the late eighteenth century by Burke. Most histories of journalism before the contemporary phase tended to an uncritical version of this account, and sought to place all of journalism within it as evidence of its contribution to the democratic process. Koss's monumental work reinforced the view that journalism was predominantly a political vehicle and claimed that the political decline of coverage of politics in the newspaper is in fact a decline in the status and value of journalism itself.

From a more critical perspective, Edelmann (1966) provided an early and exemplary view of the political context of one particular paper, arguably the pre-eminent paper of its age, the *Daily Mirror*. It is remarkable for two reasons. First, it demonstrated how a paper established a relationship with a left-leaning political party and, second, it was a paper which was not the sort of elite institution usually referred to in biographical accounts, but the leading popular tabloid newspaper anywhere in the world in its day. This account enabled further investigations of the broad political function of popular newspapers and how this formed part of their commercial appeal.

Halloran, as head of the University of Leicester's Centre for Media and Communications Research from 1966, was a pioneer of political analyses of the news media. It was one of the first academic projects which enabled investigations of how journalism constructs political events for the public, and moreover it was significant in developing rigorous frameworks for future research. The research methods developed out of this work at Leicester became significant in shaping approaches to the methodology of research across the field.

The 1970s saw political science approaches imported into studies of the relationship between journalists and their political sources in the first sustained enquiry into the much vaunted assertions that journalists were political watchdogs. Empirical enquiries such as Tunstall (1970) and Seymour-Ure (1974) led the way. Tunstall, for instance, was the first to cast a sustained and dispassionate gaze in the direction of the workings of the political lobby system, opening up a hitherto closed set of mutually reinforcing practices between elite journalists and politicians to critical inspection.

Continuing this approach to the mechanics of political reporting, Elliott (1980) looked at press performance as a political ritual while

Blumler and Gurevitch (1981) explored the role relationships of journalists and politicians and Schlesinger (1990) re-examined the role of sources in journalism.

Golding and Middleton (1982) looked more broadly at the social and political impact of the patterns of reporting poverty in the press in *Images of Welfare: Press and Public Attitudes to Poverty*. Franklin and Parton's (1991) *Social Work, The Media and Public Relations* was a milestone in the extension of political investigations into the impact of particular representations of public policy.

The work of German scholar Jürgen Habermas (1989) became a touchstone in many debates dealing with political life in Britain. It was not translated into English until 1989, a fact which delayed its impact in the English-speaking world despite the fact that its central empirical analysis was based on English periodical culture of the early eighteenth century. The driving concept of the work is that of the public sphere, a space which had been carved out to serve the rational self-interest of the eighteenth-century bourgeoisie. This under-pinned his insistence that democracies needed once again to recon-sider the ways in which their news media were responsive to the opinions of educated citizens in communicating with the power elite.

The packaging of politics thesis of Franklin (1994) has proved very influential in public debates on this perennial dialogue between the producers of political communication and its con-sumers, as too has Negrine's (1989) exploration of the processes at the heart of the contemporary professionalization of politics, which has a considerable amount of material of interest to journalism. Specific recent studies on political journalism include Muhlmann's (2008) book on political journalism, which serves to provide a broader international perspective to the history of political journal-ism, while Sparrow (2003), now the current senior political corre-spondent on the *Guardian*, has written an insider's history with great empathy for the journalists themselves.

SPIN

It has long been accepted that politicians are inevitably prone to foreground particular framings of their policies to maximize or minimize public impact. There had always considerations about whether the day was suitable for the release of good news or bad news and what were the best ways of communicating such news to the public via the news media within the communication process. What is new is the intensity of mutual suspicion between politicians and the news media. To an extent it had always been there as journalists attempted to gain access to more information than politicians were willing to disclose, and politicians became necessarily adept at constructing partial versions of the truth in a more invasive media environment. With the publication of Blumler and Gurevitch's (1995) *The Crisis of Political Communication*, based on detailed analysis of political communication over the previous decade, the authors claimed that the public were actively disengaging with a process where both parties were engaged in cynically ignoring the needs of the electorate. Accounts of spin-doctoring reached a high point as the New Labour project discovered new efficiencies in getting their message across, despite what they perceived as a news media environment hostile to their objectives. Many of these accounts were grounded in historically informed contrasts between different types of political communication management and rested on carefully observed contemporary practices. Experienced journalism and media commentator John Lloyd (2004) penned a complaint that the media were fundamentally damaging the fabric of our political system. In contrast, from an academic perspective, McNair's sensitive and accessible account of the role of journalism in establishing and maintaining democratic engagement includes an assertion that, in drawing attention to the process of political communication, spin-doctoring is not necessarily a bad thing, as it engages realistically with a critical and sceptical audience. The accessibility of this work was also important in that it exposed large numbers of students to the importance of journalism in politics. With the publication of *Journalism and Democracy*, McNair (2000) was arguing that in many ways political life had become more open through the operation of a sceptical journalism acting on behalf of the public and that in most ways public life was the better for this scrutiny. Academic investigation had by this point become an important contribution to the critique of the behaviour of both news media and political classes, with the Universities of Loughborough, Westminster, Cardiff and Leicester becoming centres of investigative analysis of many of the facets of political communication, especially around election time.

Barnett and Gaber provide in *Westminster Tales* one of the most exhaustive accounts of the centrality of Westminster to political reporting, while in contrast Cranfield (1976) and, later, Murphy (1976) and Franklin and Murphy (1991) had previously acted as voices speaking up on behalf of the importance of a provincial perspective on political reporting and its place in the democratic ecology.

FEMINIST MEDIA STUDIES INTO JOURNALISM STUDIES

This has represented an interesting but not as yet fully integrated development. Much excellent work in media studies, and often work which used news media as its analytical substance, has been restricted by the rather empirical preferences of much Journalism Studies research. Highly theorized feminist scholarship has, however, found ways to engage with the more pragmatic world of the news media and its products, including work from media scholars (Carter et al., 1998; Ross, 2001; Chambers et al., 2004; Ross, 2005). In addition there has been workplace-oriented exploration by van Zoonen (1994), Christmas (1997) and Peters (2001). Some of the earliest explicitly female-oriented research emanated from work from female scholar Gaye Tuchman (1973), who, although not a theoretically informed feminist, still coined the emotive and expressive phrase 'symbolic annihilation' to describe the subtle processes at work which removed women from the agenda of the news media, without any apparently overt discrimination. There has also been interesting reflective work from columnists who as women are in such great demand in today's news media, showing how experience can be matched to empirical and theorized research. Amanda Platell, hardly someone to categorize herself as a 'feminist', could still declare her experiences on newspapers as constituting 'institutionalized sexism' (Platell, 1999), while in the same volume Zoë Heller (1999) outlines the pitfalls of writing as a woman from within a masculine culture.

GENDER AND JOURNALISM EDUCATION

Overwhelmingly, students on journalism courses are female. This is, in part, a response to the shifting perceptions of journalism as an area of rich potential for women as employees. Journalism now offers many more posts for women than ever before, yet there is still evidence that this increase is merely providing more inhabitants of the 'velvet ghetto', while hard news and managerial posts are reserved for men. Debates are largely driven from within feminist social science approaches which can capture the empirical and ethnographic evidence of employment practice and environment as well as the anecdotal complexities of women's experience of working in the news media (van Zoonen, 1998; De Bruin, 2000).

RECEPTION OF JOURNALISM

Cultural analysis probes both the self-image of the journalist and the rituals, myths and understanding of themselves and their place in the world which journalists bring to the debate. It can also include the perception of journalists and journalism by audiences and their status as communicators. These forms of analysis stretch from film representations of journalism to opinion polls on the trustworthiness of the journalist and ethnographic surveys conducted by academic researchers on the changing professional identities of those who earn their living as journalists.

From Evelyn Waugh's (1938) *Scoop*, there has been no shortage of representation and discussion of the role of journalism in wider cultural discourse. This has even produced books on the fictional representation of journalists (McNair, 2010) written by academics, reflecting on the impact of perceptions of the role of journalists as part of our shared cultural landscape. Yet from a more empirical perspective, and related to the studies of ethical and legal issues facing journalism, there have been many surveys on the trustworthiness and reliability of journalists from Mori (Worcester, 1998) to Yougov (Barnett, 2006) which feed into general discussions and journalist-oriented discussions in publications such as *Broadcast*, the *Press Gazette*, *the Journalist* and the *British Journalism Review* on the extent to which journalism is reaching the expectations of its consumers.

One of the consequences of the wide range of discussion on the culture of journalism is that it has broadened out studies from conventional factual reports on politics or foreign affairs to include a much wider variety, including sports, celebrity and tabloid, magazines for men and women's journalism.

Goldsmiths' Unit for Journalism Research contributes to lively contemporary debate on journalism and its pragmatic dialogue with contemporary culture. Notably it brings theory and current journalists into debate and discussion. The award of a large Leverhulme grant has enabled the Unit, under the direction of notable media historian James Curran and his colleague, Natalie Fenton, to explore the empirical and theoretical implications of new media technologies for the news media. This draws upon the best in social science research traditions in investigating real-life cases of journalism's contemporary practice and has enabled lively forums for debating their provisional findings, which were enriched by a wide-ranging audience of scholars and journalists.

Good research into journalism must go beyond the anecdote and the subjective. Questions such as how long news items on television used to be; what percentage of newspapers was taken up with political news; how many special correspondents does a newspaper have; what percentage of stories are generated by PR sources: all need quantifying and measuring over time before they can be properly analysed and conclusions drawn. They provide the ultimate antidote to the 'golden age', misty-eyed view of the past sometimes provided by both producer and consumer of journalism.

THE RISE OF THE PEER-REVIEWED JOURNAL

One sign of the coming of age of any academic discipline is its ability to generate peer-reviewed journals specific to its own community of students and scholars. Large, Anglo-American publishers such as Taylor & Francis and Sage launched journals specifically in the area in 2000, with *Journalism Studies* appearing just prior to *Journalism: Theory, Practice and Criticism*. Both these journals have subsequently been increased to six issues a year and Taylor & Francis, in a demonstration of the rude health of the research environment in Journalism Studies at home and globally, launched a companion journal, *Journalism Practice*, in February 2007. *Ethical Space* from 2004 provided a regular internationally oriented forum for discussions of communication ethics, especially those concerning journalism. It was pioneered and led by Lincoln journalism professor Richard Keeble. Peer-review is the process in which work is submitted and reviewed by experts in the field who are unaware of the author of the piece under review. It is the cornerstone of quality control in the academy. Such journals assist in the fostering of coherent research agendas within the university setting, which in turn further assists the establishment of Journalism Studies institutionally within the academy and gives it greater confidence in feeding back its findings to the news industries and offering itself as a reliable source of investigation into those industries if asked to act in this way. Research can then contribute to the economic, social, cultural, institutional and practical understanding and development of journalism. As well as offering a publication opportunity for former journalists now working in universities as mature researchers, the journals increasingly afford the chance for newcomers and current journalists to review books in their areas of expertise, thus adding to the professional dialogue with research.

PUBLISHING RESEARCH

Major publishers have made publication a strategic priority, matching both the healthy recruitment of students onto the growing number of courses and the vibrant exchange of ideas in and around the new area of Journalism Studies. Journalists who have broken into academic debates contribute in publications, such as Delano and Henningham (1995) and Hargreaves (2002), have provided the benchmarks on the demographic composition of journalism and the variety of university courses on offer providing appropriate levels of education and training. Nick Davies's (2008) *Flat Earth News* is a direct illustration of the combination of academic empirical research with the more anecdotal insider observations of a prominent investigative journalist wondering where all the investigative journalism has gone! It is built upon empirical research conducted within the School of Journalism and Media and Cultural Studies at Cardiff University. Amidst an explosion of textbooks and research-led publications in the field, there was a book series launched in 2007 as Journalism Studies: Key Texts with the aim of bridging the gap between research and practice and drawing in both practitioners and academics in its authorship.

Regardless of the healthy state of research in Journalism Studies in Britain it is intrinsically linked with the particularities of higher education ecology. In the main journalism is taught as a skills-based course in over 50 universities offering over 600 combinations at both undergraduate and postgraduate levels. Research has tended to be focused within departments with traditional social science and humanities research structures at more established universities. Higher education reforms in 1992 have meant that newer vocational subjects are clustered at 'new' universities where resources and culture tend to orient journalism towards a practical route and where former practitioners are laden with heavy teaching and marking loads which prevent them in the main from producing reflective work on their own practice or a reflective curriculum which engages on behalf of students in much of contemporary research.

RESEARCH ASSESSMENT EXERCISES AND JOURNALISM STUDIES

Despite the fact that students and journalists, still less the general reader of this book, have little interest by and large in the inner workings of how research into Journalism Studies at universities is assessed, there is nevertheless a direct correlation between the perceived quality of journalism departments and the ranking of their research in peer assessment conducted on a periodic basis. When students apply to universities, and very often when journalists rate journalism departments, the best regarded and most popular courses tend to be overwhelmingly at universities with the best reputations for academic research. This draws in high-level students, high-quality academic staff and the added funding which research generates within HE. In brief, in the current funding environment the assessment of research into Journalism Studies has a tangible if indirect influence on the experience of students at university.

There have been four assessments of research quality at British universities over the past twenty years: 1992, 1996, 2001 and 2008. Formal research assessment has coincided with the growth of university-based teaching of journalism in the UK. This has provided both opportunities and impediments for the emergence of academic research specifically into journalism. Certainly within the inevitable institutional constraints, research assessment has provided a means of articulating what Journalism Studies might mean in terms of a distinctive research identity. One of the strongest contributions of the assessment of research to the development of the subject area of Journalism Studies is in concentrating work within traditions and approaches which are comprehensible to the social sciences or arts and humanities in ways which enhance interdisciplinarity and the potential for future collaborations. Nevertheless, there are aspects which could be addressed more strategically if the subject area is to use future research exercises to develop confidence and build capacity.

Generally, the criteria for assessment have remained constant to the extent that all research publications must be based within established patterns of research excellence as defined by the scholarly community. This means that work must emanate primarily from a clearly defined research question and follow identifiable patterns of research methodology. The panel within which journalism research is assessed encompasses media, communications and cultural studies. Contributions to the panel consists of books – single- or multiple-authored, or edited scholarly collections – articles in peer-reviewed journals and chapters in books. Some of these are more valued than others depending on the preferences of individual institutions and the institutional interpretations of claims of individual authors for the quality of their output, but in broad terms those playing the game most astutely become adept at developing a pragmatic approach to publication: saddling horses for particular courses.

Beyond publications themselves which constitute the backbone of the process, the research culture is an important part of the assessment of quality and also of the sustainability of research at particular institutions. Journalism research has much to offer here since, as a relatively recent addition to the research community, it has the potential to demonstrate increasing support for PhD students and the emergence of pathways which enable former journalists to reflect and contribute to research through their own accumulated experience, fused within the research traditions of the university. This remains largely in the realm of potential, however, as much research in Journalism Studies continues to be clustered around traditional universities, with staff at 'new' universities often too preoccupied by the demands of delivering practical courses to the large numbers of students imposed by institutions looking for growth.

The assessment of the research environment and the esteem of the work of individuals, groups or clusters enables a mapping of the reputation and reach of research across the international community. The allocation of research grants assists greatly in this and on occasions there are genuine synergies between research funders and vital questions of the social consequences of changes in the environment of the news media. The best possible outcome would be that institutions with high-quality outputs and well-developed research cultures within journalism research should be eligible for research funding from news media institutions as well as from state-funded or philanthropic agencies. Some of the best of this work in the UK has been funded, for example, by the Society of Editors, the Johnston Press, the Leverhulme Trust and the BBC, and has been conducted respectively by academics at the Universities of Sheffield, Central Lancashire, Goldsmiths and Cardiff.

Each new cycle of research assessment brings a twist. This time, with the newly minted Research Excellence Framework for 2013, we have 'impact'. The strangest thing is that some of the work within the broad field of Media and Communications which has the most impact is, in fact, journalism itself and yet still, it appears, this will not be eligible for submission as it does not conform to definitions of research used by the assessment panel. Researchers need to be able to construct plausible arguments as to how their work on news media has a measurable impact on wider social, political and even economic life. There is certainly a desperate need for journalists and former journalists to build an argument for the impact of certain types of journalism practice as research and in doing so follow the example of other professionals such as architects, lawyers, artists and film makers, who have been able to take the academic rules of engagement and bend them to their own purposes, explaining how research questions can work for them and be assessed in terms of peer-review and common understandings of quality. This might not be applicable to all journalism as it is not applicable to all aspects of the other examples of subject areas mentioned, but journalists working within the academy should surely be able to come to common understandings of what makes outstanding journalism and how it can demonstrate an impact.

The process of research assessment as experienced by Journalism Studies in the UK has not been without criticisms of how it has commodified intellectual enquiry and has led to accusations of cynical manoeuvring by both individual scholars and departments, yet for all its undoubted faults it remains a peer-reviewed process and therefore holds out the possibility that peers will be those who are charged with improving its operations. This is the forum within which research into the academic study of journalism in the UK is being conducted. In this author's view it offers plenty of potential for those willing to graft hard to establish a more secure footing for Journalism Studies within the academy. Despite the devil in the details of the British research assessment processes, a guarded optimist might well agree that it could be a lot worse.

CONCLUSION

Journalism Studies draws in the main from the twin strands of social science and humanities research paradigms which have assisted in its development. Research could be said to have benefited from a fuller integration with existing research models as it has moved from individual accounts, to empirical accounts, to socially integrated accounts, to more interdisciplinary accounts placing journalism within its proper multiple settings. We have shifted significantly from views of journalism as part of a hostile attack on democratic values within the Frankfurt School's interpretation. The social and the cultural context of news producers, news organizations and their impact on the 'self-evident' nature of reporting practices are now much better expressed within journalism research. Such research can illuminate the purposes and effectiveness of journalism professionally and/or explore the social meanings of journalism for/ with readers. There remains a division of views between journalism being interpreted as an emancipator or as a mechanism of political/ economic control, but within this there is room for healthy public debate.

FURTHER READING

Berger and Luckman (1967) *The Social Construction of Reality: A treatise in the sociology of knowledge*, Penguin, was a very early outing for concepts relevant to the roots of media representation, which had a wide and profound influence on subsequent studies of journalism.

McQuail (2008) *McQuail's Mass Communication Theory*, fifth edition, Sage. First published in 1983, this has largely become the market leader in the broader field of communications and is a huge influence on the narrower concerns of Journalism Studies research. Other notable examples which incorporate many of the common research methods from notable centres of communications research at British universities, and which locate potential research into journalism in a wider social science context and demonstrates that Journalism Studies research cannot be considered an island, are:

Deacon, Pickering, Golding, and Murdock (1999) *Researching Communications*, Sage; Hansen, Cottle, Negrine, and Newbold (1998) *Mass Communications Research*, Palgrave Macmillan; Franklin et al. (2005) *Key Concepts in Journalism Studies*, Sage – another book worth considering as an introduction to some of the terminology used in Journalism Studies research.

Another book which does similar work, with even more of an emphasis on presenting an international perspective, is Löffelholz and Weaver (2008) *Global Journalism Research*, Wiley-Blackwell, which considers methods and approaches to journalism research from Asia, Africa, Western and Eastern Europe, and North and Latin America.

Montgomery (2007) *The Discourse of Broadcast News: A linguistic approach,* Routledge, is a demonstration of analytical approaches to broadcast media and an exemplary application of discourse methodology to a specific form of journalism.

Richardson (2006) *Analysing Newspapers: An approach from critical discourse analysis*, Palgrave Macmillan, is a fine example of how to explore the substance and function of one form of news media language.

Wahl-Jorgensen and Hanitzsch (2009) *Handbook of Journalism Studies*, Routledge, is a panoramic view of the field, covering all the bases in the subject as it matures globally as a set of approaches to research, teaching and professional practice.

4

DEBATES ON THE PROCESSES OF JOURNALISM

INTRODUCTION

Previous chapters have indicated how Journalism Studies is a combination of research into journalism and a reflection on how journalism can best be taught within a university setting. Having looked at a general overview of the development of this combination, we will now concentrate on a particular approach within Journalism Studies, namely, the exploration of the processes of journalism. For our purposes, the processes can be summarized as the gathering, structuring and dissemination of information about the contemporary world and the ways in which these processes are affected by regulation, professionalization, political and commercial pressures, as well as by technological and cultural changes. Before the emergence of Journalism Studies as a sustained area of critical discussion, the processes of journalism had had little exposure to the outside world, beyond accounts which emerged at the level of individual newspapers or magazines or famous editors or owners, and even these tended to be unsystematic and developed in isolation. One benefit of more attention being paid to the mechanics of the processes is that changes in journalism over time can be illuminated and consequently this can enable us better to assess changes in the contemporary news environment.

PROCESS AND HISTORY

There are a number of strands of research which explore particular journalistic processes. One of the chief benefits of this research is that it impacts on both reflection and practice with implications for students of journalism, broadly defined. Indeed the question of how processes are taught and reflected upon within university curricula are matters of central importance. Discussion of how information is gathered, presented and distributed to specific audiences is central to the changing ecology of journalism. The process is, moreover, always under discussion since technologies, audiences and commercial considerations have never allowed journalism to remain unchanged or unchallenged. The process has been at the forefront of how journalism entered the modern era after the lifting of the Stamp Duties in 1885. This opened up journalism to the full force of market competition. Chalaby (1998) claimed in fact that this marketization of journalism, what he calls the 'invention of journalism', divided the process of journalism from that of previous periodical publication. Prior to this, newspapers had been more dependent for their content on the opinions and political passions of their contributors and publishers than on any need to create and maintain a commercial identity. Although one could dispute this, and make a counter-claim that all the ingredients for journalism had been present for several centuries, Chalaby is correct to point out that it was in the shift towards a fully integrated economic model of communication for particular segments of the market, as consumers rather than citizens, that journalism took shape in its modern guise. Journalism, from this point, starts to become organized as a set of more predictable routines, particularly with regard to newsgathering. The development of telegraphic communication, also from the mid-nineteenth century, meant that news was more abundant and needed to be sifted and crafted to fit the space available. The commercial drive to invest in newer, speedier technologies meant that newspapers became more reliant on advertising revenue to supplement the cover price of the newspaper, meaning that the matching of the product to the market took on a steadily increasing importance. Concentration on profits and investment in technology led inexorably to the streamlining and specialization of content, which are shaped within the modern routines of the process of journalism.

EARLY DISCUSSIONS OF PROCESS

There had, of course, been a long tradition of cultural commentary on the impact of the newspaper on society. This had become particularly prominent as the New Journalism began to reshape the market and clientele for journalism towards the end of the nineteenth century. 'New Journalism' was the term coined in the 1880s to describe the combination of layout, illustration and livelier prose which aimed at providing a more popular product for both reader and advertiser and it delivered the momentum behind the move to the first mass-market newspapers of the late Victorian era. The huge profits and mass circulation of both periodicals and daily newspapers by the start of the twentieth century had generated significant discussion in both parliamentary and publishing circles. It became common to read of concerns expressed about the influence of the press barons and their aggressive editorializing from the time of the Second Boer War (1899–1902) through the heyday of anxieties on the negative nature of press influence through the 1920s and 1930s, which culminated in the first Royal Commission on the Press (1949).

Indeed, it was from within sustained academic considerations of the changes which were ushered in by the press barons that a more considered view of what they had brought to the processes of journalism emerged. Analyses from writers such as Boyce (1986) suggested that the characteristics of the press barons were not so much a radical break between what came before this period and what followed. Instead, he argued, they sit as part of a nostalgia for a former era of perceived superiority on the one hand and as a precursor to an era of greater professional conformity on the other. The press barons form part of the mythologizing of a 'golden age' so commonly deployed by journalists nearing the end of their careers, who protest that it was all so much better in their day, so much more adventurous, more heroic. From the perspective of a social historian, Chalaby (2000) contributed a notable chapter in a fine collection of essays published on the centenary of Harmsworth's (later Lord Northcliffe) seismic shift into the modern processes of journalism which saw the launch of what was to become within a couple of years the first million-selling British newspaper, the *Daily Mail*. Most of the chapters in this volume point to the fact that the revolution which Northcliffe began was more an organizational coup than any major shift in the content of his newspaper. All that Northcliffe had done was bring existing commercial journalism into a more smoothly organized network of production and distribution and, in addition, he appreciated that this efficiency was largely dependent on the need to harness the wealth of advertising to his burgeoning audience. If Northcliffe made the process of journalism more efficient, he also recognized the tone which would appeal to readers of all social backgrounds. His success with the *Daily Mail* was so great that it determined the shape and pace of all his competitors' responses. This continued to have an impact ultimately on the way in which other news media such as radio and television were developed, as they needed to fit within the market dominance of the style of the popular press instigated by Northcliffe.

NEWS VALUES UNDER THE MICROSCOPE

The key process of journalism is the gathering and selection of information considered newsworthy. For most of journalism's history there was little in the way of methodological examination of what became news or why something was newsworthy in the first place. It was claimed, anecdotally, to be a combination of the common sense of the reporter and his/her awareness of the target audience for which the news was presented. This was linked to an increasing self-awareness of editorial identity which drove the news selection process from within the news media industries. External assessments of the patterning of these processes of selection and presentation began to set up interesting contrasts to insider accounts from the 1960s. The latter prioritized the idea of the 'nose for news' as an instinct which the true journalist had allegedly been born with. Such an explanation ignored the socialization and institutional context within which the journalist had to operate, that is, the socio-economic patterning of the newsgathering process prioritized by the academic investigators.

The most influential academic study of news values is surely that of Galtung and Ruge (1965). Despite its rather narrow focus on the reporting of peace news in Scandanavian newspapers, the transferability of this research to other topics in other national contexts has shown it to be an extraordinarily resilient and perceptive model. It is still often the first port of call for anyone doing an analysis of the news. Indeed most recent explorations still take it as their point of departure in studies of the news values of newspapers (Harcup and O'Neill, 2001) and broadcast journalism (Brighton and Foy, 2007).

Whereas Galtung and Ruge concentrated mainly on the procedural mechanisms which enabled certain news items to be privileged over others, other studies combined insights into the routinization of news values with their broader potential political implications. Halloran et al. (1970) used such frameworks to analyse a demonstration against the US military presence in Vietnam and were able to conclude that the television reports they studied acted in such a way as to frame the event as a violent confrontation, instigated by the protestors. They argued that this framing was constituted through the process of editorial selection in the sequencing of the pictures, which served to highlight violence apparently being instigated by the demonstrators.

NEWSGATHERING

Various studies have explored the process of newsgathering, which had hitherto remained a largely tacit sequence of decisions, adhered to by professionals and lacking anything in the way of explicit confirmation to the public. The patterns of routine and the economies and efficiencies they bring when attempting to impose editorial coherence on coverage of both expected and unexpected events began to be explored from the 1970s, with increasing deference to what had developed as a culture of journalistic tradition.

Tunstall's (1971) *Journalists at Work* was seminal in its sustained exploration of the working practices of journalists. It was based on a wide range of interviews combined with participant observation and it provided a sympathetic portrayal of the tensions and competing pressures brought to bear on the journalists and editors who shared a genuine commitment to informing the public. It served to move critical appreciation of the process away from a reliance on the instinct of individuals which most journalists acknowledged was in any case a gross simplification of the process of newsgathering; at the same time it broadened the appreciation of the complexities beyond the cliché of the 'nose for news'.

Golding and Elliott (1979) aired misgivings about many of the assumptions expressed by broadcast journalists concerning issues such as professional distance and neutrality. They observed that organizational norms and political expectations could actually be said to be compromising the ideal of public service autonomy in Britain and concluded that there was strong support for the interpretation that broadcast news was 'a systematically partial account of society' (1979: 1).

Taking up the baton from Tunstall's groundbreaking work, Burns (1977) was involved in sustained participant observation at the BBC in the mid-1970s for his book-length study *The BBC: Public Institution and Private World*. This too stressed the institutional and professional constraints which shaped the news. A slightly later work, but one which is nevertheless considered a very influential study, is Tumber's (1982) work for the British Film Institute, *Television and Riots*, which is also located within the same methodological tradition.

Once newsgathering had become established as a suitable subject for sustained study, related issues such as gatekeeping, editorial selection processes, the political self-censorship of journalists – especially on matters relating to national security – and overt editorial control all became scrutinized by professional researchers keen to explore the processes of journalism as a variation of the public interest rationale of journalists themselves. One might say that watching the watchdogs had become fair game and in its defence it was serving a reasonably clear civic agenda.

THE PARLIAMENTARY LOBBY

This was once one of the most tacit of journalism's processes, the channel through which political information was accessed in Westminster by representatives of the major news media. It originated in 1884 when concerns about civil disorder were addressed by the closure of the members' lobby of the House of Commons and only journalists on a list approved by Parliament were allowed to attend. It bore all the identifying features of a well-honed ritual of mutual self-interest and welcomed neither scrutiny nor outsiders. It came to comprise over two hundred named political correspondents from national and international newspaper, radio and television organisations. These were provided with daily briefings by senior politicians and in exchange were trusted to maintain the anonymity of sources and not to expose the behaviour of politicians within Parliament. Once critical studies began to cast their light into the process of the lobby, it was clear all was not as democratically accountable as it might have been. Kellner's (1983: 281) early broadside in *Parliamentary Affairs* accused the system of producing 'lazy journalism undertaken by lazy journalists'. Cockerell et al. (1984) continued this exposure by asserting that lobby journalists exchanged privileged access to the superficial for the right to dig deeper into areas which spokesmen would prefer to guide them away from. Journalism Studies brings together academics and political journalists to yield more consistent, probing results which can better expose the limitations of contemporary coverage, the benefits of the system for responsible journalists, as well as the potential for better. Barnett and Gaber (2001) provided one such account in *Westminster Tales*. The *Guardian*'s current political correspondent Andrew Sparrow's insider account (Sparrow, 2003) goes a long way to explaining how the system has evolved over time with all its pragmatic compromises, frailties and possibilities for further reflection. It demonstrates the polemic potential of historical accounts for practices which had been hitherto plagued by assumption and implicit, unspoken knowledge.

NEWS PROCESSES AS RITUALS

Sociologists out of the American tradition of deviance theory used news coverage as a test case for exploring how news production could be explained as a sort of ritual with a pattern of tacit expectations. Once the plausibility of this account had become established, the role of the news media in the process of social stereotyping could be better explained. Such stereotypes were never articulated as an editorial policy but developed rather as an inevitable byproduct of the construction of audiences. After all, if news media acknowledge that they deliver consumers to advertisers and, especially in the case of the BBC, an audience constructed predominantly around the concept of a national audience, it would be odd in the extreme if they did not craft their news output towards the stereotypes expected by their audience at least to a certain extent. The advantage of such explorations was that they went beyond the immediate intention of the journalist or even the editor of individual stories, to consider the shaping and patterning of a spread of news items as they related to particular issues such as youth, 'race' and gender. Early thematic work provided accounts of the clashes between the Mods and Rockers (Cohen, 1973) which claimed that the reporting went far beyond the literal relation of events to express much of broader society's anxieties about generational change while pandering to a stereotypical portrayal of youth. Cohen and Young's (1973) *The Manufacture of News* was an early exploration of the pressures brought to bear, commercially and politically, on journalists and journalism to produce news which ultimately conforms to dominant sociological perspectives. The book concentrated on the representation of deviancy and the impact of the images which were given prominence by the news media. Such approaches meant that journalism was being taken very seriously as a mode of shaping public perceptions of social activity and in defining both acceptable and unacceptable behaviour.

What united these studies was that they claimed that the processes of news production were relaying more than information; when approached with analytical insight they could be interpreted as providing a frame within which accounts could be placed with additional cultural and political emphasis. This enabled critics to revise common-sense perceptions of the news as a mirror on the world and to highlight, in contrast, its part in the mediation of social change and, most often, resistance to such change. What was of particular interest in the 1960s and 1970s was that these analytical explorations were undertaken at a moment when a newly invigorated youth culture was fashioning a very different world. However, these early sociological explorations were not related from a neutral perspective but from the strongly held political persuasions of the sociologists undertaking the research, and it was this, more than the insights themselves, which led to much hostility between the two camps of committed left-wing critics and professional journalists. Subsequently, Journalism Studies began to take a more dialogic position, drawing upon both journalistic and academic discourses to engage on these issues with a greater amount of consideration for both critical and practical perspectives which ultimately can lead to greater sensitivity in how issues are represented now that the news media know that someone is analysing the longer narratives that they purvey. The development of the role of the readers' editor, most notably at the *Guardian* from 1997, is an important part of this reflection on the processes of news selection.

TECHNOLOGY AND PROCESS

The adaptation of the daily routines of journalism to shifts in technology and the corresponding demands of the expanding range of news media from radio to the internet have provided rich sources of exploration for scholars, and these, in their turn, have delivered key contributions to studies of journalism. The processes of radio and television news production have been covered more completely presumably because, being driven by varying ideals of service to the public, they are more often judged analytically against how they measure up to such ideals.

Some of the earliest studies emerged from cultural work on the technology of broadcasting, such as Smith's (1973) *The Shadow in the Cave*, Williams's (1974) work on the technological implications of television and the more traditional archival historical work of Briggs (1961, 1965, 1970a, 1970b, 1995) on the BBC, has spanned several decades in its contribution to public knowledge about the decision-making processes at the BBC. The government-sponsored Third Royal Commission on the Press (1977) played an important role in concentrating minds on the relationships between journalism and its political-economic institutional settings. Its conclusions ultimately provided a formalization of institutional enquiry into the processes of journalism.

Attempts to understand what processes were at work in the gathering, selection and presentation of news for television developed in Britain along the lines of the work of American sociologists such as Gaye Tuchman (1973). The most notable work which contributed to this tradition came from Schlesinger, whose study of the routines of the BBC provided an influential ethnographic study of newsroom practice in 1978. This set the standard for similar ethnographic work, which sought to place the decision-making processes involved in making the news within broader understandings of both social constraints and expectations as well as the institutional demands of public service broadcasting.

The processes of newsgathering and particularly the ways that the organization of newsrooms has adapted to changes in the technologies available has seen significant work produced which draws upon the close ethnographic observation established in the 1970s. This involves tracing the movement of journalists and managers throughout their working practices and interviewing them about those activities. This of necessity generates reflection upon the distinctiveness of the working environment and the culture which the participants work within, as well as explicit acknowledgement of the role of the interviewer/researcher in the process. Ursell (2001, 2003) is worth mentioning in this context. She demonstrates the tensions between the potential of technology to provide the quality content which journalists aspire to and a commercial environment driven by profit alone.

Other notable contributions have come from Esser (1998), Harrison (2006) and Hanitzsch (2011). The location of this work within what have quite rapidly become trusted traditions of ethnographic research and the adherence of such work to high levels of ethical consideration have combined, meaning that newsrooms are more receptive to the observation process and are also increasingly likely to find the results of researchers of interest in providing possible solutions to the demands of a changing environment for the news media.

PROCESS AND PROFESSIONALIZATION

Journalism has had a problematic engagement with the concept of professionalism. On the one hand, it is reasonable to expect a certain level of truthfulness and accuracy in news reports. On the other hand it is difficult, particularly within a profit-driven market, for news to select and restrict entry to practitioners if they have material to sell. To compound this situation, the legitimate practice of wrestling important information from reluctant hands in order to expose wrong-doing in high places can easily be confused with the pursuit and publication of material which is of sensational value alone. A related problem is that information which in the first instance seems merely of value in titillating an audience might actually have a greater resonance for democracy. An oft-cited example is the *News of the World*'s coverage of the Profumo scandal in 1963, when the sexual antics of a government minister were interpreted by the press as a having implications for state security as he was sharing a mistress with a Soviet naval attaché – a fact which might plausibly have meant that secrets of state were being shared with a diplomatic enemy at the height of the Cold War. The very processes by which journalism is produced, seeking information outside the circles of respectable society, of necessity often run contrary to the environment and networks which are normally associated with the very bourgeois notion of professionalism.

The National Union of Journalists (NUJ) has a history of considering the impact of ownership and levels of staffing on the production of the news. It was instrumental in providing the first formal set of principles which attempted to establish protocols of behaviour in the process of news production in its Code of Conduct in 1936. This has been influential in establishing the parameters of process during a period when broadcast news was developing a public service philosophy from the 1930s to the 1960s.

PROCESS AND ACCESS

As journalism began to be opened up to external scrutiny of its processes, people started to expect more explicit explanations of how one could get work as a journalist and, beyond this, how to make progress in journalism as a career. Men and women from various backgrounds wanted more overt indicators of what they needed to do in order to fulfil their aspirations and potential. This scrutiny began to expose the fact that the workforce of journalists did not reflect the diverse nature of the society whose needs journalism was supposed to be serving. It was a rather closed area of employment where the only true answer to how to get on seemed to reside in who you knew. This was clearly a waste of much true talent and reinforced the notion that journalism was a cultural and professional milieu too detached from the demographic realities of modern Britain.

INCLUSION OF WOMEN: CHANGES IN NEWS

The increasing numbers of women involved in journalism has generated its own strand of exploration. First, this came in the form of memoirs of women who had struggled to enter the male domain of journalism, which was as dominated by the concerns of masculinist tendencies towards professionalism as had been the case in all of the other more formal professions which had emerged through the nineteenth century. This tradition stretched from Hulda Friedrichs's (1911) account of the life of one of the pioneers of the New Journalism, George Newnes, in the 1880s as the woman who had provided much of the interview material for Stead's *Pall Mall Gazette*; Mary Grieve's (1964) account of her life in magazines; more contemporary accounts of Sebba (1994) and MacGregor (2002). Amanda Platell's (1999) and Zoë Heller' (1999) personal accounts are of note in this context for their insistence that sexism is still rife despite a change in numerical representation and the rise of 'women's' writing in the press. Despite the value of such personal testimony, any strand of systematic discussion which sought to develop a wider perspective on these issues emanated from within the academy but more particularly from within feminist media studies. Here we see an excellent demonstration of how the scrutiny of scholars such as van Zoonen (1994, 1998) based on a range of sociological and organizational studies have begun to blend with the experiential work of former journalists drawn into the teaching of journalism in universities. Studies can now provide rich synopses of what had hitherto been fragmented accounts which could have been shrugged off as mere hearsay, sour grapes or the elevation of isolated negative experiences. The best of this work, starting with Carter et al. (1998) and most recently Chambers et al. (2004), asks hard questions about the processes which operate to exclude or marginalize women even as their numbers increase within journalism.

The processes of decision-making which had become internalized and routinized by experienced editors and reporters have come to be scrutinized in all their complexity by researchers. As journalism educators reflect in turn on their own practice, this can also begin to have an impact on the gendered processes at work in journalism.

SURVEYS OF THE RECRUITMENT PROCESS

The quality of journalism and its ability to deliver to an increasingly diverse population are highly reliant on recruitment processes which ought in principle to encourage a representative workforce. For that reason, research into these processes and the subsequent composition of the workforce are as often driven by forces inside the news media as by academics. Surveys and analyses of the workforce and sponsored explorations of the processes of journalism education and recruitment have become of great interest to insiders, yet, left to its own devices, it is unlikely that journalism would have moved at all to redress some of the imbalances in its employment practices to ensure that the news is gathered and delivered by a workforce which bears some resemblance to the audiences it purports to represent. Social and political pressures to provide evidence that equality of opportunity is taken seriously within journalism have meant that there have been structural adjustments to recruitment and promotion processes. Such scrutiny from both the inside and the outside is necessary to alter what had become extremely entrenched patterns within the workplace for female journalists.

The first wide-scope exploration was provided by Delano and Henningham (1995), and Delano followed this up with a more narrowly focused piece on women journalists in 2003. Research sponsored by the Society of Editors (2004) confirmed the lack of ethnic diversity in local newspapers serving ethnically diverse communities, while the Sutton Trust (2006) produced an equally searing indictment of the reduction in opportunities for young adults from working-class backgrounds as journalism moved increasingly towards being an upper-middle-class occupation. At the other end of the demographic spectrum, it is not a question of recruitment but of retention, which is increasingly highlighted in terms of diversity. Ageism has combined with sexism in a very public exploration of the employment practices at the BBC in the Miriam O'Reilly case in 2011.

Ainley (1998) had already examined the problems faced by black journalists even if they got work within the news media on account of its predominantly white, middle-class institutional expectations well before Greg Dyke, as Director General, observed that the BBC was 'hideously white' in an interview on BBC Radio Scotland on 7 January 2001. Francis (2003), in the *British Journalism Review*, written predominantly for an audience professionally involved in journalism, produced a brief update of how little journalism has changed despite its appointment of more prominent journalists from ethnic minorities.

WAR REPORTING

One of the many challenges faced by journalism's claims to impartiality, balance and fairness comes from its positioning within the discourses of national self-interest in times of war. You don't report against the patriotic grain! Knightley (1975, 2004) was the first to provide a comprehensive survey of the role of the war correspondent, asserting that truth was the first casualty of any conflict. He analyses the coverage of conflict from Russell's accounts of the Crimean War (1853–56) through the Falklands (1982) to the 2003 invasion of Iraq, and deals with the issue more comprehensively than anyone before, setting the standard for the many studies which have followed. It is a fine example of how productive historical accounts of journalism's processes of information gathering can be, as they show the methods of colluding with state-determined political agendas and how each armed conflict overseas continues to be explained unquestioned in the news media as vital to the security of the nation. Knightley's account generates deep scepticism about the patriotic battle cries of the news media and demonstrates that objectivity is extremely difficult to maintain in such circumstances.

There had always been an implicit security frame to studies of the news media and this became more apparent as greater scrutiny was directed towards the processes of the news media especially in times of military conflict from the introduction of D-notices in 1911. The complexity of reporting in the twentieth century has intensified as issues of political acceptability, management of crisis, prioritization of national sovereignty, self-censorship, restraint from criticism of troops or military leadership when they are in combat have become bundled within accepted norms of news media engagement. It must find a balance between the imperative of the military to restrict sensitive areas of disclosure and the countervailing imperative of journalists to report a more independent version of the truth. War reporting has become perhaps the ultimate arena in which journalism's moral duties and the high ethical claims for its own distinctiveness can be tested. The Falklands War was used as the test bed for contemporary politically acceptable access. Morrison and Tumber (1988) *Journalists at War: The Dynamics of War Reporting During the Falklands War* provided a thorough analysis of this coverage and its longer-term implications for journalism although they were working very much in the disciplinary field of sociology.

Keeble's (1997) *Secret State: Silent Press* is notable for several reasons, most evidently for the fact that it emerged out of the doctoral thesis of a prolific and high-profile journalist who had hitherto published *The Newspapers Handbook* (Keeble, 1994), which had been one of the key educational texts and one which highlighted journalism's ethical imperatives. This ethical dimension has now progressed to a well-developed strand of the author's work and is a key component of the delivery of journalism education at the Lincoln School of Journalism. Keeble developed this anti-war stance by looking at the assumptions woven into the routine language of what he terms 'massacrespeak' (Keeble, 2005a), building on Chilton (1982) on 'nukespeak' during the Cold War. To counter some of the routine aspects of war coverage which attempt to hold positions of institutional neutrality and balance, Martin Bell has become a very public advocate of a 'Journalism of Attachment' (Bell, 1998) and has delivered lectures at a number of British universities on this and related matters.

Technology has not fundamentally undermined the traditions of collusion between state and media in time of war. In fact, it seems to have entrenched them further. Technology delivers, it does not necessarily explain. This is nowhere more pertinent than in war reporting from the telegraph to handheld images of the 'war on America' of 9/11.

Post-Falklands there has been a refinement of the exploration of these processes referred to as 'embedding'. These provide harsh critiques of the work of the news media as they fulfil their patriotic imperatives at a time when the state is under military threat, real or constructed. Miller (2004), in *Tell Me Lies: Propaganda and Media Distortion in the Attack on Iraq*, provides a necessarily polemic counter-argument to common assumptions about the neutrality of news media reports on the Iraqi conflict. Tumber and Palmer (2004) have explored recent developments in the institutionalization of war reporting in the Western news media and its trade-off between access and autonomy. These have been complemented from a more global perspective by the work of Thussu and Freedman (2003) and Allan and Zelizer (2004), while Cottle (2006) has broadened out the analytical base of war reporting to include more general aspects of conflict.

TERROR, CRISIS

Undoubtedly, the news media have played a significant part in constructing contemporary understandings of terrorism. Schlesinger et al.'s (1983) *Televising Terrorism* was an early example of sustained critique of mainstream coverage of the issue in the UK. In the new century, terrorism is now once again a live subject and yet better technology has not led to any improvements in the sophistication of its coverage. Actually there is less journalism, especially less live commentary, on the sorts of conflict which drive terrorism and little in the mainstream on dissenting views on its background. For example, within news media organizations, how much debate is there on the fundamental accuracy of the oft-cited phrase 'war on terror'? It seems rather to have been adopted as uncritically as military and politicians have handed it down as a catch-all for some of the most intractable conflicts of our era. In contrast, the current critical environment has seen probing collections of perspectives from a critical perspective, notably Zelizer and Allan (2002).

REGULATION

Outside adherence to the normal laws of the land, the press is exempt from external regulation. Newspapers and magazines in contemporary Britain claim to self-regulate in accordance within the views and tastes of audiences. Justifications for such self-regulation has been refracted through circulation figures and the requirements of advertisers. Broadcasting, on the other hand, both publicly funded and commercial, has always been subject to overt, external regulation. Although debate on regulation was always theoretically in the public domain in government documents, real debate on the structure and substance of broadcast news has only really come of age with empirical studies and substantiated media commentary. Producers' guidelines were first published in 1993 as a contractual statement of the BBC's journalism philosophy, among other things.

They are a public statement of ambition and intent and they also provide a starting point for explicit engagement between critical commentators and the Corporation.

Both press and broadcasting were less exposed to sustained scrutiny before the emergence of sociological studies of the news media and before concerns about the overall quality of provision started to be tested through specific academic studies. As regulation of the broadcast media has become lighter and newspapers have become more intensely profit-driven, so academic studies and commentary from within the news media by practitioners with long memories have coincided to provide accounts questioning the sustainability of a quality press or quality broadcast news (cf. Greenslade, 2004; Petley 2006, 2008).

An interesting forum for discussion of broadcasting policy has always been the McTaggart lecture at the Edinburgh International Television Festival. This, however, was only of passing interest to media followers before it was collated into an authoritative, edited collection by Franklin (2005) for a comparative assessment of longer-term trends. Before this, there had been the Franklin (2001) *British Television Policy: A Reader*, which had gathered the wide selection of documentary evidence and critical discussion vital for longer-term considerations of policy developments.

PRESS COMPLAINTS COMMISSION

One area where newspapers have been drawn towards some common set of guidelines is through the Press Complaints Commission (PCC). This was set up in 1991 after government enquiries decided to make a last attempt to encourage newspapers into some voluntary code would prevent compulsory regulation of their content. Snoddy (1993), as media correspondent of the *Financial Times*, gives a good set of perspectives from both the insider as well as the infuriated and frustrated commentators on what could have been a dance to the death if editors of national newspapers – particularly, but not exclusively, the tabloids – had not agreed to the recommendations of the Calcutt Enquiry to ensure that they were not drinking in what had been coined as the last-chance saloon and that they were able to regulate their own excesses. Frost (2004) has provided a very useful overview of the adjudications of the PCC in its first decade and Bingham (2007) has given an account of the Calcutt Committee's aftermath. Scepticism that the PCC is at best a worn sticking plaster on a more deeply troubled area of the news media has a fine articulation in Jempson and Cookson (2004), which scrutinized the PCC, and such scepticism has only deepened since the launch of the Leveson Inquiry.

DEREGULATION

Independent bodies such as the Campaign for Press and Broadcasting Freedom, founded as long ago as 1979, have been joined by an association of concerned journalists, media lawyers and politicians in Mediawise. It was started under the name of Presswise in 1993 to protect the public from media abuse and intrusion and to highlight the ethical responsibilities of journalism to the public. It has subsequently broadened its brief to respond to what it perceives as the inexorable marketization of news media, especially the previously protected areas of public service broadcasting provision. O'Malley's (1994) *Closedown* was a powerful argument against the continuing erosion of quality provision at the BBC and this has been extended into the new century as critical responses to the work and limited remit of Ofcom from articulate critics of the structural challenges of media deregulation (Petley, 2006, 2008).

MEDIA EFFECTS

Ever since the invention of printing there have been heated debates about the influence of mediated information. In Ben Jonson's play *The Staple of News*, at the dawn of print news media in the early seventeenth century, the playwright lampoons the gullibility of the new audiences for printed news, portraying them as believing anything they see in print, overwhelmed by its novelty. This took a more urgent turn in the 1920s and 1930s as totalitarian regimes appeared to use the mass media to great effect as tools of propaganda. The Frankfurt School developed a range of influential critiques of the political and social power of the media, which fed into many common-sense anxieties. One of the benefits of wider critiques of any straightforward models of media effects is that they provide at least a more subtle approach to the audience and credit the consumer with a lot more selectivity and power than earlier syringe models, in which an audience is 'injected' with media messages, as though through a hypodermic needle. The passive audience has generally been argued out of the frame and has been replaced by reception studies which allow for more autonomy in how the audience interprets the messages of the mass media. Even so, there are still influential studies of how news media agendas can set up particular cultures of reception which match existing audience preconceptions (Critcher, 2003).

IMPARTIALITY

The statutory obligations of broadcast news media to provide information which does not editorialize and which provides balance between opposing viewpoints and attempts to act as an impartial source of information have been enshrined from the start within broadcast journalism in the UK. Debates about these high ideals and what starting points there might be for achieving them have evolved at the same pace as the process of investigating certain of journalism's core claims. Wilson (1996), for instance, pointed out the impracticality of any definitive version of the 'impartial' in *Understanding Journalism: A guide to issues*.

IN-HOUSE PUBLICATIONS

There are several publications of note which have contributed over the years to a full range of discussion of journalism by journalists. The *Journalist*, produced by the NUJ, was first published in November 1908 as the *National Union Journal* before changing its title in 1917. It has taken on a more critically engaged perspective as practitioners have moved with increasingly regularity between the news media, critical commentary and the academy. This means that journalists are writing much more as critical commentators on their own practice and on the nature of the news media industry. This trend is noticeable also in the *Press Gazette*, first published in 1965, and *Broadcast* (1959), both written for industry insiders and full of considered reflection.

In 1989 the *British Journalism Review* was established 'to help journalists reflect on the changing character and problems of their job' as articulated in its inaugural issue. It dealt and continues to deal with issues of concern to the journalists from the ethics of confidentiality to phone tapping and the shortcomings of contemporary regulation frameworks for broadcast journalism. In addition, its book reviews can provide an interesting industry encounter with academic publications.

TABLOIDIZATION

One of the most heated discussions within the contemporary news media is on the perceived process of tabloidization. This is a term coined as recently as 1992 for a process which has been evolving since at least 1901, when the first named tabloid newspaper was launched as a one-day stunt by Harmsworth and Pulitzer on the latter's *New York World* newspaper. This process could claim to be nothing less than the story of twentieth-century journalism, as it has had an all-pervasive influence on its form and scope. The language and style of first the popular newspaper in Britain and then the tabloid have had a steady impact on newspapers generally over the past hundred years. Not only have broadsheet newspapers been driven for commercial reasons to adopt a 'compact' format but the emphasis and style of the language of these newspapers have been orientated more towards the news values of the tabloids, as these newspapers all try to emphasize their congruence with popular culture in an era of unprecedented competition in the media. This process may not be a one-way street, however. It may be, as Bromley and Tumber (1997) have speculated, that, after the gradual convergence of tabloid and broadsheet styles, a process of respecialization may see different newspapers (particularly in their online manifestations) starting to diverge considerably in their tone, style and coverage once again.

TABLOIDIZATION: PROCESS OR PANIC?

The history of the twentieth century's journalism has been a struggle between the forces of commerce and the interests of the people. Tabloidization may be the extended working out of the process of commercial logic within journalism. Although tabloidization is a problematic label which includes the organization and production of journalism as well as just format in its terms of debate (Esser, 1999), the tabloid popular papers have been the pioneers of the trend. Although the sensationalism and personalization of the popular press have long been the subject of discussion and complaint on a national basis, particularly in advanced capitalist democracies, what has happened over the past twenty years is that a combination of political, cultural and technological changes have triggered a set of ripples which have spread across national as well as media boundaries to cause a range of debate about how processes once confined to the lower end of the market are now perceived to have infected the whole media landscape. As concern has spread, within the elite news media, political circles and parts of the academic community, the perception of the acceleration towards 'tabloidization' has become a moral panic in its own right (Gripsrud, 2000: 287).

Sparks (2000) identifies three ways in which the term is used to identify shifts in the boundaries of journalism; shifts within the priorities of journalism; and shifts of tastes within media forms. Paletz (1998: 65–8) has identified four trends within tabloidization which impact upon subject matter: priorities concerning content; forms of presentation; journalistic techniques; and ethics. Tabloidization may therefore refer to an increase in news about celebrities, entertainment, lifestyle features, personal issues, an increase in sensationalism, in the use of pictures and sloganized headlines, vulgar language and a decrease in international news, public affairs news including politics, the reduction in the length of words in a story and the reduction of the complexity of language, and also a convergence with agendas of popular and, in particular television, culture. Tabloids are characterized as being primarily to do with a combination of format and language: 'editorial matter is presented in emotive language in easy-to-consume formats' (Rooney, 2000: 91). It is clearly, if nothing else, an impressive growl-list of elements, some of which have haunted the minds of commentators on journalism over centuries.

As the panic unfolds, the perceived process of 'tabloidization' has begun to move beyond the description of a particular kind of journalism to become a general description of what is regarded as the trivialization of media content in general (Turner: 2004: 76; McKee, 2005). This tendency is exaggerated because the process is not restricted to the tabloid newspaper but is connected to a more complex set of changes, a 'dynamic structural transformation' within the whole media sector from the introduction of new technologies to general social changes (Sparks and Tulloch, 2000: 160). Maybe it represents part of a broader 'communication chaos' (McNair, 2006: 552) enveloping and perhaps threatening the whole of journalism in the twenty-first century.

To its critics, tabloidization signifies an inexorable decline in journalistic standards; to its admirers or even its pragmatic observers, it represents an amalgam of professional and economic compromises with the realities of contemporary popular culture which has successfully colonized much of the spectrum of journalism in the twenty-first century. Dahlgren (1992) suggested that journalism should be considered as part of, not separate from, popular culture, and indeed the tabloidization of journalism is such an important feature of contemporary trends in the culture at large that we could say that tabloid culture can no longer be conveniently quarantined in an annexe some distance from the concerns of mainstream or even elite cultural activity.

CONCLUSION

The processes of journalism have been shrouded for a long time in misunderstanding and even mystery. Nevertheless, there are long-standing concerns about how journalists go about producing the content of journalism, and Journalism Studies has attempted to provide as comprehensive a view of those processes as possible. These explorations have drawn historically on longer narratives of concern about how journalism is affected by the ownership or regulation of its various outputs. A key question is whether the producers of journalism can be considered as professionals in the light of the importance of journalism to democratic debate. Studying how regulation and deregulation have impacted upon the processes of journalism can help us understand how it functions both routinely within a capitalist economy and within exceptional circumstances like war and perceived terrorist threat. Matters of taste, the relationship of journalism to other popular media cultures and journalism's claims to be a communication form distinct from public relations have also been explored through a range of scholarship. Sociologists have constructed models of the rituals and traditions of the newsgathering process and this has been used as the basis for work which explores how news value is understood both inside and outside the news media industries themselves. Longer-term information-gathering and empirical study have helped us to understand how recruitment to journalism and certain of its traditions has prevented a more representative workforce from emerging. Just as an awareness of the longer-term historical interest in journalism as process sheds light on journalism's core qualities, consideration of the impact of technology helps us to understand how these processes have been shaped in the past and are being reshaped by new developments in its contemporary phase. All of these strands of exploration have enabled us to make more sense of the distinctive nature of journalism's multiple and changing processes.

FURTHER READING

Further accounts on the processes of journalism emanating from universities and which aim to give students critical insights into the ways that contemporary journalism functions include:

Biressi and Nunn (2007) (eds) *The Tabloid Culture Reader*, Open University Press. This is a wide-ranging collection of views on the ways in which tabloid culture is produced and reproduced within a range of media including journalism.

Chambers et al. (2004) *Women and Journalism*, Routledge. This is a wide-ranging assessment of research into the state of the roles and traditions of women within what has often been seen as a very patriarchal industry. It highlights the gains and the limitations of women's engagement with journalism and is informed by all of the relevant historical and sociological research.

Conboy (2006) *Tabloid Britain*, Routledge. This argues from a perspective which prioritizes the ways in which the popular tabloids could be said to produce the modern nation of readers.

The whole Media Skills series from Routledge, including works on reporting, writing, interviewing, writing for broadcast journalism, magazines, feature writing, radio broadcast journalism.

Hemmingway (2007) *Into the Newsroom: Exploring the digital production of regional television news,* Routledge. This is a fine account by a former BBC journalist of the changing environment of television news, with unique levels of access to journalists and newsrooms at a local level.

Niblock (2006) *News Production: Theory and practice,* Routledge. Bridging theory and practice and drawing on exemplary ethnographic research, this provides an absorbing account of the production processes in the contemporary newsroom.

Sparks and Tulloch (2000) *Tabloid Tales*, Rowman and Littlefield. This includes both critical exploration and journalists' accounts of the importance of tabloid journalism around the world.

Witschge, Phillips and Lee-Wright (2011) *Changing Journalism*, Routledge. Looking at current practices in the UK and overseas across media and technological platforms and embracing a wide range of methods including interviews, ethnographic research and content analysis, this is a bold attempt to capture something of the challenges and excitement of current processes. In doing this it manages to combine both practitioner insight and theoretical reflection.

5

PRODUCTS

INTRODUCTION

Journalism is an increasingly complex form of public communication so it is no surprise that the end product of its various processes has generated significant reflection. Much of this relates to changes in the products; the potential for changes in journalism for new markets; the broadening of expectation in relation to the quality of the product; and the shifting social and economic uses of journalism as part of a spectrum of media consumption. These generate debate at legal and political levels as well as at public and professional levels and these are increasingly refracted through the academic lens provided by Journalism Studies.

INFLUENCE OF OWNERS ON PRODUCT

There have long been suspicions of the influence of individuals on the content of journalism, ranging from the press barons of the early twentieth century to more contemporary media moguls. From major media characters from the late nineteenth and early twentieth centuries such as Northcliffe, Beaverbrook or Rothermere to more familiar players of recent years such as Maxwell and Murdoch, all have had genuine ambitions regarding their own personal powers of persuasion and the potential for real political influence to be mediated through their news products. However, within the complex processes at work in the news media, it is debatable if they have had any direct influence on consumers despite their sometimes well-documented impact on their editors. This has not prevented politicians, cultural commentators and indeed journalists from bemoaning the personal impact of these owners on both audience and product. Sustained studies on ownership and control have brought us more nuanced and better informed analysis of the dynamics and motivations within complex communication processes from the broader perspective of the political economy of journalism. Australian journalist turned academic David McKnight (2003) has brought us highly persuasive accounts of the complexities at work between Rupert Murdoch's personal and political beliefs and the changing structure of his business model. Informed insiders such as Greenslade (2004) or Chippendale and Horrie (1992), Marr (2004) or MacGregor (2002) draw upon a body of critical literature and respond to questions posed by it in framing their own accounts of the news media. More sustained explorations of the political economy assert that it is the profit motive of all news media which ultimately determines the shape and content of mainstream journalism. The first significant work in the field came from Garnham (1990). This has been reworked for contemporary audiences by work on the structures of contemporary media ownership by Doyle (2003) and Cottle (2003). The latter is keen to explain the role of cultures of production within the profit-driven environment of news media. Such explorations informed by established research paradigms offer an example of how self-critique, emanating from within journalism, has moved on to become a significantly more sophisticated set of responses than it once was.

CRITICS OF THE PRODUCT: THE LONG VIEW

There have been discussions about the quality of the content of our news media since the beginning of periodical publication in England in the seventeenth century. Once low standards were the accepted norm. Gradually more came to be expected of journalism. Concerns about declining standards are now able to be quantified and sometimes even challenged in ways which can be measured against anecdotal evidence. Sometimes the common-sense view of things is not necessarily a very accurate assessment and journalism can even come out with its reputation enhanced.

In order to establish some common ground for understanding the very public issue of what constitutes good journalism, there have been constant discussions between the journalists themselves, social and political commentators and members of the audience throughout journalism's history. Where the area of Journalism Studies has had an impact is in creating a space in which these sort of discussions can become more formalized, more quantifiable. This has been of particular use in exploring and dismissing various claims concerning 'golden ages' of journalism (Rooney, 2000; Tulloch, 2000) as contrasted with the biographies of great men and certain narratives of press and broadcasting history which overemphasize the achievements of the past. An excellent example is Scannell and Cardiff's (1991) privileging of the social context of radio which moves early broadcast journalism very much away from the personal influence of powerful managers and politicians. Debates on the decline in journalistic standards, the emergence of 'tabloidization', the impact of news media stories on the perceptions of danger in society, concerns about sensationalism in the press or the role and value of Public Service Broadcasting are among the hotly disputed issues which will be covered in this chapter.

BROADCAST JOURNALISM

Unlike the press, broadcast journalism has always needed to adhere to monitored standards of coverage. This remained the same with the advent of commercial television from 1955, despite the fact that former Director General of the BBC, Reith, was famously reported to be of the opinion that commercial television was as much to be feared as the bubonic plague. There are well-documented accounts of concerns within contemporary newsrooms about the combination of new technologies with commercial pressures on the quality and depth of television news coverage. For instance, Jon Snow (1997), the presenter of Channel Four news, considers that the steady reduction in time allocated to each news item on television news is destructive of previous levels of journalistic quality. The issue of declining standards in television journalism has been scrutinized by several academics, including Bromley (2001), Winston (2002), Barnett and Seymour (1999). However, their findings are not as conclusive as one might expect. More often it has been observed that patterns of presentation have actually remained more constant over time than is supposed. Commitment to 'impartiality' and adherence to topics regarded as of interest to the public still remain high on the broadcasters' agenda. Even when the forces of competition leak in from other media forms, there are more elastic approaches to questions of the quality of the product presented to the viewer such as Langer (1998) and Harrington (2008), who see such changes as an accommodation to the realities of a world in which news media form part of a more general mediatized world with inevitable crossovers and consolidations with other media.

On Public Service Broadcasting we have seen a long series of government-sponsored Commissions, Broadcasting Acts and discussions leading most recently to the founding of Ofcom in 2003. At the BBC there have been concerns whether the Corporation adheres to its own principles of best practice, which led to both the resignation of its Director General, Greg Dyke, and the Hutton Enquiry. From the academic perspective we have critiques from O'Malley (1994) to Petley (2006, 2008) and Barnett (2006) and the rise of the Mori and Yougov polls to ascertain what the public think of the services produced for them by their news media. Here we can witness a shift in concern from the content of programmes in themselves to the political and legislative context of programming and a highlighting of the perceived dangers of neoliberal preferences for market-driven solutions to the provision of public service journalism.

THE CHALLENGE OF THE DIGITAL WORLD

In the here and now, many people are concerned about journalism itself across all platforms under the impact of new technologies, social media and a shrinking advertising base. Particularly within commercially based news media, there is alarm that without a sustainable economic model of journalism there will be a growing democratic deficit between what we need to know to function within a democracy and what is available as a common resource for debate on the important political issues. The blurring of boundaries between journalism and social media appear to be exacerbating this, particularly among young media consumers. Important work is being produced by a range of academics, which is feeding into debate within the news media themselves. The best examples are the appointment of a Chair of Digital Media at the University of Central Lancashire sponsored by the Johnston Press and the three conferences on the Future of Journalism/Newspapers held by Cardiff University with participation and interest from a range of news media commentators and practitioners. Where the area of Journalism Studies has demonstrably had an impact is in creating a forum for these discussions to become more aware of each other. It was heartening to see a large grant dedicated to the question of what sort of news is being generated by new media. The Leverhulme Trust sponsored work at Goldsmiths, University of London, which drew on case studies, ethnographic research, empirical data and interviews with the current journalists, and this was eventually published as *New Media: Old News*, edited by Fenton (2010), and *The Death of Auntie: the tragic decline of a great institution*, by Lee-Wright et al. (2012).

Conferences and special issue publications of peer-reviewed journals have certainly helped to make the study of the range of factors which influence contemporary journalism much more intensive. This is of particular importance in trying to disentangle rumour from fact, pessimistic assertion from identifiable trends in a reliable and quantifiable form when it comes to assessing the impact of new practices on the current products of journalism.

PUBLIC RELATIONS

One of the major contemporary discussions on the product of journalism relates to the relationship between journalism and public relations. There is a widespread perception among both journalists and commentators on journalism that public relations is increasingly dominating news media agendas as journalists themselves come under pressure to produce results quickly and efficiently without leaving the office and without going through some of the procedures of checking and corroboration which would have been automatic even twenty years ago. Academic studies have helped shed light on the incrementalism of this process and its broader political implications from Davis (2002) to L'Etaing (2004), as well as Julia Hobsbawm's (2006) counter-challenge to journalism to up its game! Franklin's (2009) dictionary of key concepts in public relations assists in providing a much needed introduction to the professional terms and critical vocabulary of a practice often derided as the very opposite of journalism.

Such is the importance of this dialogue, between what many have traditionally viewed as mutually hostile practices, that it may well define whether journalism, as we have come to understand it historically, continues to survive as a communicative form. Baistow (1985) was prescient in identifying the growing influence of the public relations industry upon the substance of journalism. This came, in his view, as a consequence of the increasingly mediated political sphere, particularly under the influence of broadcast television's representation of politics and politicians' responses in carefully framing their media performances and spending much more time on the representational aspects of their communication strategies. The influence of PR on journalism has led many to explore the claims and counter-claims of the protagonists. Journalists had long proclaimed a superior mission to that of the public relations professionals but now the latter claim that in many cases they are complementary to the product that journalists purvey and sometimes even more authoritative. Davis (2002) argues that this has had a negative effect on the political integrity of independent journalism and there are further related questions about the quality of journalism given the PR-inspired moves towards 'spinning' the communication of politics (Oborne, 1999; Jones, 1995). To be fair, this media analysis has been countered by the man some see as the master of spin himself, Tony Blair's Director of Communications, Alastair Campbell, who maintained that what politicians are trying to achieve is to get their message through a profoundly sceptical news media machine which is working against the public's need to know. There has been interesting work (Salter, 2005) which highlights analytically the differences between journalism's goals and those of PR. He claims that they simply work to the demands of different logics which can never be combined. Against the protestations of journalists that they seek out revelations and provoke conflict and discussion rather than the search for closure of messages around predetermined corporate agendas, there is the evidence that journalists are becoming more re-processors and recyclers than generators of stories. This has led to articulate pleas for journalism to re-engage with a field which has become, for many, much more complementary to journalism in recent years (Hobsbawm, 2006).

JOURNALISM STUDIES AND THE TEACHING OF HOW THE PRODUCT IS CREATED

The rise of formal studies of journalism at university level has created an important reconsideration of the production of journalism from a systematic viewpoint. We have already looked at the formalization of journalism education but here is an opportunity to consider the growth of publications which seek to disseminate a more reflective account of how the product comes about. This draws upon the experience of many former and some still practising journalists and has led to the emergence of a level of consensus on what needs to be taught. At first, as we have seen in our account of education, a purely imitative process led to the ingestion of the best way to arrive at the finished product. Clearly this left room for criticism that it was too passive and conservative a process, which led to an unreflective reproduction of a particular sort of journalism, leaving any change which did occur down to the accidental incursion of external forces. The best that literature on the subject got was a series of amateur books aimed at the enthusiast, such as *Teach Yourself Journalism* (Candlin, 1951). There were exceptions, though, which drew on the experiences of former prestigious journalists, such as a five-volume series of books on editing, language and design of newspapers published between 1973 and 1978 by Harold Evans, the former editor of the *Sunday Times* (1967–81).

The formalization of journalism education begins a cavalcade of opportunity for expositions of how to produce good journalism. The first notable book is surely Richard Keeble's (1994) *The Newspapers Handbook*, which epitomized the need to provide students with a guide which was embedded in experience as well as pedagogy, practice as well as reflection. It set the standard for books which provided an authoritative account of how to arrive at a finished product which met the highest standards of which journalism is capable. The thrust of Keeble's book led to other volumes which gave an equal emphasis on the how as well as the why of various forms of journalism, from broadcasting to magazines, and some which also collected essays by notable practitioners guiding students through the varied forms of journalism such as, once again, the wonderful exposition provided by Keeble (2005b) in his *Print Journalism: A Critical Introduction*. Another example of a book which has managed to inculcate a fine demonstration of what is practically required in combination with an astute assessment of the political and cultural contexts in which journalism is produced and consumed is Harcup's (2004) *Journalism: Principles and Practice*.

Andrew Boyd's (1988) *Broadcast Journalism* was for many years the first and most influential text in its field and one which taught students what they should be doing and what it meant to be a broadcast journalist. The acceleration of publications has meant that there is now a steady stream of books aimed at students and their lecturers, most notably the series Media Skills edited by Keeble, especially the volume outlining the basic and also finer points of interviewing produced by Beaman (2000).

The only downside is the crowding of the market by publishers who are often keen to make an easy killing. This is aggravated by the unwillingness of the news media industries in general to compile their own preferred readings which best identify what students need to know and what context they require. This has led to the publication of some books which seek to simplify the complex set of considerations which go to create the finished product. Some publishers continue looking for the El Dorado of a practice book which will be bought by all students as a one-stop text – an unrealistic goal, but it doesn't stop them trying.

MAGAZINE JOURNALISM

Long after newspapers became objects of study, and even as broadcast journalism began to attract critical attention, magazines remained by comparison a neglected field. This is strange from one perspective, since magazines constitute the largest sector of the journalism market by far. Yet, from another perspective, this neglect is easier to understand. Magazines are closely entwined with consumption and with the domestic or personal space of fashion choice, hobby and leisure. Their distance from the world of politics and high culture meant that they were little scrutinized in themselves. They were sometimes addressed as conduits to better understanding of domesticity (Beetham, 1996) or the representation of women (Adburgham, 1972) but less so as journalistic products in themselves. This started to be addressed across the spectrum from exposition to critique and they are now just beginning to be given the attention they merit. Early accounts of magazines had sometimes assessed the production of magazine journalism and its place within journalism in general. The best known of these accounts from a British perspective was White (1970). Later the question of what was actually produced, how it was consumed (Hermes, 1995) and the economic structure of the product were explored in McKay (2000) and Gough-Yates (2003) and the language specific to magazines in McLoughlin (2000). A broader consideration of the magazine genre was provided in John Hartley's (1996) iconoclastic review of the role of the magazine in *Popular Reality*. They have recently been the subject of three international conferences based in Cardiff, driven by the organizational energy of former magazine-journalist-turned-academic Tim Holmes. The 'Mapping the Magazine' conferences (2003, 2005 and 2011), the first partly sponsored by the British Academy, which indicated the serious cultural interest in the field, demonstrated what a diversity of forms magazines had taken and the breadth of critical perspective which could be used to engage with them both historically and in the contemporary world. The first two conferences led to the publication of a special issue of *Journalism Studies* (Holmes, 2007). Consideration of a view of the magazine as a female genre was challenged by the emergence of studies on the new men's magazines, which have become as profitable as they have been culturally intriguing, from Stevenson et al. (2001) to Benwell (2003). From this point onwards the education of students gearing themselves towards the possibility of working with magazines was going to be able to provide as rich a context to the creation of the product as broadcasting and print have been doing for some time.

TABLOID CONTENT

Like many of the developments of twentieth-century journalism, the tabloid had its roots in the nineteenth century. A little exposition here will do us no harm! The pharmaceutical company Burroughs Wellcome and Co copyrighted the term 'tabloid' in 1884 to advertise their marketing of compressed medicines in the form of small tablets. The term itself is a contraction of 'tablet' and 'alkaloid'. It was on New Year's Day in 1901 that the first copy of a tabloid newspaper appeared. Harmsworth had been invited by Pulitzer to New York to oversee the production of an experimental, one-off, tabloid-sized version of his *New York World*. He showed his appreciation of the commercial appeal of the instant news digest when his slogan boasted: 'All the news in sixty seconds'. Presciently, he announced that it would be the newspaper of the century. In retrospect, we can see that this was not hyperbole but an accurate assessment of the future of not only the newspaper but increasingly of journalism in all its formats. Although the *Daily Mirror* (1903) and the *Daily Sketch* (1908) preceded it, the first newspaper which we would recognize as tabloid in format as well as content was the *New York Daily News* in 1919. It provided an early combination of the sensation, brash sexuality, bold headlines, human interest and sport that would come to identify the tabloid genre.

The tabloid as the most overtly populist of products has attracted some of the most interesting reflection on the substance of journalism and it has adapted to the intense commercialization of the late twentieth century. Yet the roots of the tabloid precede this recent intensification. It was the *Daily Mirror* in 1934 that triggered the so-called tabloid revolution, with its signature heavy black bold type for its headlines, pin-ups, young style, simplified language and a prominent use of pictures to reach a new readership. Curran and Seaton (1993: 53) have argued that this constituted a 'key moment in the incorporation of the popular press by the entertainment industry' with its slashing of political, social and economic news to formulate a newspaper of appeal to the working classes. It redefined and then dominated the market with a proletarian language of specifically commercial appeal (Bingham and Conboy, 2009).

It soon generated a certain biographical and political scrutiny, first from managing editor Hugh Cudlipp (1953) and then from Edelmann (1966) in perhaps the most astute reading of the political impact of a popular paper to that point.

THE *SUN*: RESTRUCTURING THE POPULAR PRODUCT

The most significant, recent development in the history of British tabloid journalism was the relaunch of the *Sun* in 1969. Thomas (2005) provided a nuanced view of the general relationship between popular tabloids and the Labour Party, which might have expected high levels of support from newspapers aimed at the working classes. He argued that the rationale behind the relaunched *Sun* dramatically altered these expectations. The epoch-defining pitch for a new, downmarket popular newspaper lay in Murdoch's conviction that that the *Mirror* had become 'too posh for the people' by the 1960s. By the mid-1960s, Cudlipp had begun to reposition the *Mirror*, if not upmarket, then certainly towards a more serious readership, with features such as 'World Spotlight' and 'Mirrorscope'. Under editor Larry Lamb, Murdoch set out to produce an alternative that was explicitly based on an updated version of their rival's irreverent approach of previous decades. Lamb (1989) himself recounts how he scrapped all specialist news reporters except political journalists and specialized in human interest, sensation and sex, significantly narrowing its news agenda. The *Sun* targeted younger readers, dropped the increasingly serious ambitions of the *Mirror*, embraced the permissiveness of the age and provided a disrespectful, anti-establishment, entertainment-driven agenda. It reinforced its popular credentials by exploiting television advertising and by providing an intensified interest in the off- and on-screen activities of the characters in soap operas on British television. From his perspective as deputy chief sub-editor on the paper, Greenslade has summed up its impact in the following overview:

> the *Sun* had shown that there was an audience for softer, features-based material and heavily angled news in which comment and reporting were intertwined. It also adopted a more idiosyncratic agenda, presenting offbeat stories that fell outside the remit of broadcast news producers. It cultivated brashness, deliberately appealing to the earthier interests – and possibly, baser instincts – of a mass working-class audience.
>
> (Greenslade, 2004: 337)

What made the *Sun* distinctive was its ability to transform the language of populist appeal away from the *Mirror*'s left-leaning progressive brand of politics to a new articulation of the sentiments and policies of the right, which was identified by political commentators as an 'authoritarian populism' (Hall and Jacques, 1983: 22) Its effect was contagious to many areas of the press, with its rabid anti-union stance becoming a perspective maintained by most of the national newspaper press (Marr, 2005: 169). It soon perfected a style of vernacular address which highlighted the perceived interests of a newly articulated blue-collar conservatism. This was, however, nothing new to some more historically informed commentators such as Seymour-Ure (2000: 23) who observed: 'Ever since its birth, the popular press has bolstered capitalism by encouraging acquisitive, materialistic and individualistic values.'

Kelvin MacKenzie, the editor from 1981, encapsulated this new mood perfectly. His preferred slogan was 'Shock and Amaze on Every Page'. Chippendale and Horrie (1992) provided a racy account of the rise of the paper and in particular the role of its most successful editor. Fiercely patriotic and a staunch supporter of the Conservative Prime Minister, he was always unequivocally supportive of British military involvement.

The paper was also important in terms of its sexual politics. Holland (1983) provided a subtle reading of how the news agenda of the paper and its raucous appeal formed part of an endorsement of the potential of pleasure in the lives of working-class readers, presenting itself as the champion of sexual liberation, albeit of a particularly narrow, heterosexual, male-dominated variety. This particular paper's attitudes towards sex were what came to define the popular journalism of the age. Tabloid content became even more pronounced in a more intensely competitive market. It seemed as if, as Snoddy (1993) has discussed, the race was on to find the bottom of the barrel in terms of public tolerance.

The *Daily Star*, launched in 1978, beat the *Sun* by a short head in the plummet towards the lowest tolerance point in the late 1980s in the sexualization of popular culture (Holland, 1998). It attempted to provide the *Sun* with its nemesis but it failed. It has been described as having 'a circus layout that fairly burst from the pages ... the paper used more italics, more reverses, and more graphics in conjunction with sensational heads and stories to give a sense of excitement and power' (Taylor, 1992: 45). Engel (1996: 17) comments that each generation of successful, popular newspapers has been undercut by a new wave which has been able to capture the readership of a lower social grouping and integrate that readership within the widest range of appropriate other media such as advertising, cinema and television. The *Daily Star* certainly attempted to outperform the *Sun* in this respect in the basement of tabloid taste. It was aimed at the lowest end of the market in terms of sex, sensation and dubious journalism ethics, with an appeal to an even younger market than the *Sun*. Its limited success meant that, with sales falling and advertisers withdrawing contracts by the early 1990s, the paper stepped strategically away from its policy of 'bonk journalism', thus demonstrating how continually coarsening their content does not guarantee the next generation of popular newspapers' success. It was almost entirely the fault of the tabloids in their pursuit of the bottom of this barrel that the Calcutt Committee into Privacy and Related Matters was set up as a last attempt to encourage some sort of responsibility from newspapers short of imposing legislation which would encroach upon the freedoms the press had come to take for granted. In 2000, an edited collection entitled *Tabloid Tales* (Sparks and Tulloch, 2000) made the case that tabloid culture had permeated news media across the world. Its introduction explained clearly why this journalistic phenomenon was clearly the most important journalistic product of the age, because of its ability to cross borders both of geography and taste as well as in its ability to provoke moral outrage.

TABLOID SHAPE

The first key developments in the tabloiding of British newspapers are defined initially and literally by the shift of the *Sun* to a tabloid format in 1969 and the *Daily Mail* in 1971. The *Daily Express* completed the middle market shift to the format in 1977, the *News of the World* from 1984 and *Sunday Express* went tabloid from 1992. The next stage was the reformatting of most of the elite press – styled as 'compacts' – with the *Independent* leading the way in 2004 followed by *The Times* and the *Guardian*'s shift to the slighter larger 'Berliner' format in 2005, leaving now only the *Daily Telegraph* and the specialist *Financial Times* holding out as genuine broadsheets in the daily market.

Beyond the downsizing of the former broadsheets, it is alleged that they have also been increasingly affected by tabloid style and news values. McLachlan and Golding (2000) have charted the growth in visuals in relation to text as one indicator of the impact of the tabloid product, squeezing text out of the frame. Other strategies which conform to the tabloid model, according to their study, have included the inclusion of more lifestyle and consumer coverage, and an increasing number of journalists being granted the media star treatment with a photograph accompanying their byline and allowed freer rein to write from a more personalized perspective. Tunstall (1996) argued, even before their reformatting, that objectivity on elite newspapers had shifted considerably towards more of a house-style orientation than anything absolute and he interpreted this as part of their need to differentiate themselves within the media market, to take the style of coverage further than regulated broadcast media are permitted.

Thomas (2005) argues that there is a direct correlation between aspects of the development of tabloid newspaper language and their reporting of politics which has drifted into the elite press as it has come to depend on the populist techniques of the tabloids to maintain their position in an increasingly competitive market. This has meant a move away from balanced reporting, positive, politician-centred communication to a more negative, journalist-dominated approach and to one-story front pages, screaming headlines and short, punchy campaigning prose at the expense of more detailed text or long quotations from politicians. In this sense, Thomas claims, the tabloid medium certainly has affected the message, while Marr concludes that the consequent tone of mocking scepticism, adopted almost as a contemporary default within journalism, has eroded the credibility of democracy (Marr, 2005: 71). Critics of these trends which are so characteristic of the reporting of political life in Britain see the shift towards sensation, emotion and scandal as a major element in what amounts to a crisis in public life: 'the negation of the kind of journalism that is essential to democracy' (Sparks, 1998: 6).

Within the newspaper industry itself, there is a clear acknowledgement that the trends towards tabloid strategy as well as tabloid content and format are well advanced: 'Since the 1980s broadsheet newspapers have adopted many of the commercial, as well as editorial, practices of the tabloid press, including promotional stunts, cover price discounts and brand exploitation' (Greenslade, 1996: 17).

More recently the editor of the *Guardian* (Rusbridger, 2005) has highlighted that it is the way that quality newspapers in Britain continue to adapt to the pressures of this commercialized and tabloid-influenced market which will define the next generation of serious newspapers in this country, while McNair sees changes in the content and style of the elite press as a positive move towards a more inclusive, even democratic, journalism culture: 'Less pompous, less pedagogic, less male, more human, more vivacious, more demotic' (McNair, 2003: 50).

A further endorsement of the encroachment of tabloid style on the elite press comes from Peter Preston, a former editor (1975–95) of the *Guardian*. It benefits from a longer historical perspective than many critics can provide:

> The truth – my dawning truth from 1976 – is that tabloid actually suits the current broadsheet news and feature agenda best. It's the natural way of seeking to address segments of a readership which itself is increasingly composed of segments. It forces editors to put their judgement on the line. It establishes its own priorities, not an order of news nicked straight off the 6 *O'Clock News* on the BBC. Tabloid is much more than easy reading on the Tube. It is a means to a disciplined end, a clarity of mind.
>
> 'What took us so long, then? Why was it the autumn of 2003 before *The Independent* broke the British mould?'
>
> (Preston, 2004: 51)

THE TELEVISION BULLETIN

The BBC has always attempted to construct as wide a national audience as possible, chiefly to justify its public funding, although the tone of its address has shifted considerably from paternalist to populist over the century. This shift was in part because of the increased competition for the loyalty of the popular constituency ushered in by the introduction of ITN in the 1950s. From this period, the format of television journalism has expanded from set times and a singular style to accommodate changing viewing patterns, and a plurality of styles have been developed to address different audiences at different times of the day. Within this proliferation, the imperative has become to popularize the product so as to best justify expenditure and retain market share. The first experiment in adapting television news to changing patterns of consumption and lifestyle was regular breakfast television news in 1983. This saw a shift in the hitherto rather austere image of the newscaster. These journalists, easy on the eye and with tones suited to a new style of 'sofa journalism', were very different creatures to their counterparts in other broadcast news programmes. Breakfast television news introduced a softer range of human interest angles on stories in the news and because of its man–woman double act it was dubbed 'Ken and Barbie' journalism (Van Zoonen, 1998: 40). In the wake of breakfast television news, the presentation and formats of mainstream television news went through a process of rapid transformation. Regional journalism began to become more oriented to a lighter style, with more human interest and good news stories. Within prime-time mainstream news there was an increased use of text on the screen, a sound-bite syntax which reduced the length of individual news items. The use of graphics to illustrate news and the increasing informality of newscasters and reporters are all indications of the popularization of television news.

In November 1992 ITN's *News at Ten* was relaunched in a new, visually more dynamic format, with one newscaster rather than two and a greater emphasis on 'human interest' in its stories. The BBC went for more populist approaches to 'difficult' stories as part of a radical reappraisal of news and current affairs ushered in by Director General John Birt (1992–2000). As a summation of these trends in mainstream commercial news programming, Channel 5 News was launched in April 1997, fronted by the photogenic Kirsty Young and targeted specifically at an audience of 'younger adults'. It has been observed that it aggressively advertised its innovativeness in paying more attention to positive news stories, and incorporating more human interest and lifestyle coverage into its programming (McNair, 1998: 117).

Barnett and Gaber (2001) concluded that ITN and Sky operate to a more identifiable tabloid agenda with shorter items, more sport, celebrity-based stories and less foreign reporting, while BBC TV and radio continue to adhere to a more serious one. This has been reinforced by comparative research (Kadritzke, 2000), which contrasts the greater contextualizing and informative character of

BBC news against that on commercial channels, which is distinguished by its busy and personable style, its broad range and, in many items, its shallowness (Ursell, 2001: 192). Yet the BBC has not been immune from moves to follow the populist aesthetic trends of commercial news providers in preferring more visually appealing television newscasters and reporters. This has embroiled the Corporation, in line with commercial rivals, in arguments over the suitability of older women as newsreaders, in particular when Moira Stuart resigned in 2007, as it was alleged she was fearful of being moved out for a more photogenic and younger replacement. The logic of more aesthetically pleasing TV presenters seems to fit within a general movement of broadcast news towards entertainment values and may even represent a part of a bid to retain appeal to a younger audience which is turning off from mainstream news and politics.

Winston (2002) conducted research which suggests that claims that there is a convergence of television news to a 'tabloid' format are not borne out in any generalizable way. Longitudinal studies, he argues, demonstrate that changes in television journalism are more complex in their editorial shifts and emphases. There have been changes in emphasis and presentational style but the content has not moved consistently in any particular direction. However, Barnett and Seymour (1999) do conclude that the drift to lighter content and more human-interest-driven presentation and theme is borne out if we shift our focus from news bulletins to current affairs journalism and documentary more generally. The most notorious example of this was when *Tonight with Trevor McDonald* replaced *World in Action* in 1998 as ITV's only current affairs programme. Current affairs programmes such as this, drawing on the celebrity status of its anchor, are symptomatic of an increased management perception that television journalism must appeal as widely as possible to maintain a popular appeal regardless of the quality of its content.

CELEBRITY CONTENT

Celebrity is increasingly used as a 'hook' to snare readers and viewers into journalistic offerings or as the main attraction in itself. Tabloid culture has mushroomed to the extent that it has an impact even when the elite press are drawn into condemning the constant coverage of celebrities. Such tabloid tendencies to cross-reference celebrity and entertainment issues can be witnessed increasingly as part of the repertoire of the elite press and broadcast journalism in all its forms and are part of a strategy to reach new audiences in a crowded market and a changing cultural environment.

Controversy notwithstanding, celebrity journalism poses questions familiar to journalism: questions about the worth and significance of social developments; questions about the place and function of public communicators; questions about the balance in our news agenda between the serious and the trivial.

Celebrity journalism provides a broad, rich and often disturbing panorama of the characters of contemporary life. The specific historical nature of capitalism may mean that 'celebrity' is a very different economic and cultural category than its predecessors, fame and notoriety, but the appeal of coverage of persons in the public gaze has lost none of its lustre or financial incentive to the news media. Marshall sees celebrity culture as part of a process which is 'widening the public sphere' (Marshall, 2010: 40) but Turner (2004: 82–5), in pronouncing it a 'demotic turn' rather than a necessarily democratic one, remains sceptical that the fascination of the media with the everyday is anything more than an astute representation of media oportunism rather than any genuine enhancement of the media's democractic functions.

A more generalized tabloid culture (Biressi and Nunn, 2007) represents Britain as a community of interrelated media celebrities and amplifies this with a style of language which matches that culture. The tabloids not only report on the lives of celebrities; they use this information to enhance as many stories as they can with a plethora of intertextual references to them. On the one hand, it may be claimed that this 'democratizes' the news, moving it away from its traditional insistence on the elites of society and a preponderance of political and financial reports, yet, at the same time, it may also limit the reach of the news agenda and continue to restrict the people who register as 'elite persons' (Galtung and Ruge, 1965) but in different ways.

Connell (1992) claims that celebrity coverage acts as a commentary on the disparity between social classes and the resultant gulf in wealth in Western societies which does not find an expression elsewhere in our mediascape, concluding that the popular tabloids have generated a necessary if limited awareness of the matter. We might add that, since Connell provided this insight, celebrity has diversified to act as a prismatic view on contemporary discourses on gender, sexual morality, politics, national identity, mental health – in fact most aspects of contemporary life. Nevertheless this coverage falls well short of any critique or commentary and remains restricted to a melodramatic moralism (Gripsrud, 1992). A notable recent example was when a winner of £9.7 million on the National Lottery, Michael Carroll, an ex-binman, lost all of the money in a short period of reckless spending and investment. He was regularly castigated in the blue-collar *Sun* as 'Lotto Yobbo', in effect demonstrating that he had been given an opportunity which was unsuitable for one of such lowly status, and on 29 April 2005 was dubbed the 'King of the Chavs' by the *Daily Mirror*. Coverage across the tabloids included his anti-social behaviour, court appearances, bad taste in clothes and fondness for brash displays of wealth. Almost by definition a case of the undeserving rich, it provided an inverted fairy story for our age – a rags to rags story very much in the narrative shape of other modern celebrity morality tales. Celebrity news is a perfect conduit for the tabloids, as it allows the fluid interchange between fact and fiction as well as the easy generic transfer from information to entertainment (Hill, 2005: 15) upon which their values are centred.

FROM NEWSZACK TO McJOURNALISM

Before 'tabloidization' there was Malcolm Muggeridge's accusation that we were being provided with newszack akin to the bland and homogenized background music provided in supermarkets. Franklin (1997) takes this up to provide a full-scale commentary on the decline of overt political news. According to this analysis, competition, lighter broadcast regulation, new technologies which have destabilized traditional career trajectories and the perception that audiences want entertainment rather more than they want information have all combined in a toothless, dull and mediocre contemporary journalism product.

Claims that tabloidization has all but eroded quality journalism at the local level are more substantively borne out given the collapse of the local small ad market and its migration to the internet, leaving an increasingly impoverished product. Here, Franklin (2005) has borrowed the conceptual framework of the McDonaldization thesis from Ritzer (1998). This is a graphic account of how the products of local journalism have become homogenized in order to keep costs down while maintaining profits and by delivering a journalism which is high on identifiable similarities across regions but low on any genuine originality or insight: as profitable and as bland as a burger.

ROLLING NEWS

The latest combination of innovation and format in television journalism is 'rolling news', where cost-conscious managers have exploited an opportunity to deploy technology to provide more quality for less. This is now considered a desirable component of any broadcaster's output (Cushion and Lewis, 2010). Rolling news first appeared in the UK with the introduction of the commercial radio station LBC in 1974. Sky introduced a British version of the American CNN format in 1989 and the BBC soon followed suit. The main substantiated criticism is that it provides more speculation rather than information, a criticism that is echoed in complaints from senior broadcasters themselves about 'systematic sloppiness' (Leslie, 2004: 12).

ROYAL COMMISSIONS

The Royal Commissions on the Press were in large part concerned with the product of journalism. The three Commissions, which reported in 1949, 1962 and 1977, had a variety of motivations and purposes, but common to them all was an overriding concern about the quality of print journalism. It was widely perceived that the political content of newspapers was too dependent on the ownership and political preferences of a narrow group of owners for it to represent the broader range of opinion needed for full democratic engagement. Despite their deliberations it is hard to make any claims for long-term impact.

INVESTIGATIVE JOURNALISM

Investigation is certainly a central part of the process of journalism, looking in places where others are disinclined to look! Yet it can also be considered as an end product of journalism. This is the area which most concerns traditional supporters of journalism in its watchdog role. This is another product within the range of journalism which is liable to be castigated as being in decline though often from a perspective lacking much in the way of hard evidence or empirical research. The methods of producing such a complex and potentially dangerous form of journalism need even more careful consideration than mainstream journalism, so it was welcome to see the publication of the summative experiences of experienced reporter Hugo de Burgh (2000) in a book which started consideration of the possibilities and pitfalls of the investigative product.

Of course, all good journalism involves an essential element of investigation, so 'investigative journalism' is to an extent a tautology. Nevertheless, a particular form of journalism out of the tradition of 'aggression and access', which had been imported from America in the mid-nineteenth century, was first exploited as campaigning journalism by the pioneer of the New Journalism and editor of the *Pall Mall Gazette*, W.T. Stead, and then in the twentieth century was employed by quality newspapers and television teams to expose serious corruption. The heyday of investigative journalism was in the 1960s and 1970s, as newspapers and television companies vied for the reputation of being the most diligent public watchdogs. The tactics of investigative journalism have often been deployed by the popular press for sensation alone. Indeed, the current Leveson Inquiry highlights how much investment popular tabloids have made in investigating the trivial over the last decade.

There have been a number of studies exploring the decline of primary investigation within journalism. These have ranged from studies of print journalism to the decline in the quantity and quality of investigative reporting and current affairs programming on mainstream television. The answer in both cases is that investigative journalism is expensive at a time where cutting costs is becoming the primary driving force within journalism. Barnett and Seymour (1999) from the University of Westminster provided the hard evidence to support claims that current affairs television was dealing with less original investigative work because of the restructuring of production budgets. Nick Davies (2008) draws upon extensive research conducted at the University of Cardiff which has established in a quantifiable way how the product is less likely to have been generated by traditional investigative journalistic input these days. Despite the decline Sparks (2000) has demonstrated that there is a niche for the traditional skills of this aspect of journalism's repertoire to be formally taught.

LOCAL JOURNALISM

The local variant of journalism so central to the establishment and maintenance of political and economic communities down the centuries has not attracted its fair share of scrutiny. From a critical perspective this has most often come from writers exploring historical perspectives such as Cranfield (1962) or Aldridge's (2007) sociological approach. From a career perspective local journalism was seen too frequently as merely the route into something more prestigious, and certainly into something better paid. There is little directed towards the local product from a practical perspective and this would appear to be linked with the tradition that dictates the apprentice should merely learn by doing at that level without too much in the way of specialization or reflection. There is some consideration of some of the routines of local journalism within the textbooks, but in the main these skip quite quickly to skills which can be more broadly applied to the national product.

At a critical level there has been something of a revival. This has been driven by work emanating from early explorations of the practice and traditions of local journalism by Murphy (1976) and Franklin and Murphy (1991). Much of this work was predicated on the assertion that local political life was enriched by the quality of local journalism. There was much evidence to support this view and much pessimism concerning the direction in which local journalism was heading. O'Neill and O'Connor (2008) have observed many of the trends affecting mainstream national journalism having an influence on the content and scope of local practice. Matthews (2013) promises an interesting new take on the history and contemporary challenges facing the local press.

One of the issues which emerges from technologized and hyper-capitalized journalism on a global scale is that it is very hard to make profits from something as narrowly focused as local journalism. It certainly has its political perspective and certainly can draw on the energies of local enthusiasts, but the business model upon which it had depended for so long is falling away, with no replacement in sight. Interestingly enough this calls for a new model of local engagement through the traditional aspirations of journalism as a source of local identification and a conduit for the discussion of local political issues. Journalism Studies is attempting to provide a range of reflection which can also be applied to devolved national news media which face a similar set of economic and cultural challenges, from Barlow (2005) to Blain (2008) and transnational assessments such as Cushion's (2010) report on reporting devolution.

BROADENING OUT DEFINITIONS OF JOURNALISM

As the content of journalism has been studied more systematically and as its range of content has diversified from a concentration on the delivery of the latest information to commentary, opinion – even speculation – there has been an increase in exploration of the boundaries of journalism. The subsequent cultural environment has encouraged productions which question the generic conventions of journalism, including some of its core claims.

Following on from the tradition of satirical journalism best demonstrated in modern times by *Private Eye*, since1961, there have been a variety of subversive comic attacks on the forms, conventions and traditions of television news and the documentary form itself. This has been most successfully and controversially executed by Chris Morris, first on the radio with *On the Hour*, which later transferred to television as *The Day Today* in 1994. Yet his finest satirical hour was to come with *Brass Eye* in 1997, when he mocked the standard coverage of controversial topics such as drugs and most notoriously paedophilia. More recently still, this satirical tradition has been extended in the crossover between stand-up comedy and journalism by proponents such as Mark Thomas and Jeremy Hardy. Current news satire shows which use the news and its presentational styles for comic entertainment include the long-running *Have I Got News for You*. *2DTV* was an animated news satire which ran from 2001 to 2004 on ITV and in a similar vein we have *The Late Edition* on BBC Four.

Gordon Burn's (2008) novel *Born Yesterday: The news as a novel* relates the experiences of a protagonist who witnesses a series of interlocking news events strangely woven into his own experience of another, parallel world. Both of these are presented as narrative strands which threaten to converge but ultimately resist any resolution. News follows and informs novelistic conventions until the observer has difficulty disentangling what and who is real in a contemporary hall of echoes. It is a timely piece of reflection on the ways that journalism has become almost instantaneously part of different, overlapping discourses of entertainment and intrigue, for example, in the main narrative in this case which deals with the spin-offs from the disappearance of Madeleine McCann.

These sorts of hybrid variants of journalism reflect the richer cultural context of news today. There is more interactivity and more communication between entertainment and informational forms as journalism struggles to maintain its own absolute position as information provider under pressure from online sources and amateur enthusiasts.

ALTERNATIVE JOURNALISM

There have been many accounts of the possibility of alternative approaches to journalism notably in the work of writers and activists keen to stress the radical potential of including the perspectives of the working classes or other groups excluded from the attentions of the mainstream press. These were often produced by political or literary critics and one of the most influential was Harrison's (1974) *Poor Men's Guardians*, which provided an overview of historical attempts to provide a press which was not reliant on the machinations of big business or the interests of the political elite. Accounts more firmly rooted in the practice of journalism have included recent work by Atton and Hamilton (2009) and studies of alternative means of addressing social issues such as that pioneered by the *Big Issue* (Swithinscale, 2001).

CONCLUSION

One might say that a perception that the product of journalism is in crisis is in fact the normal state of affairs. This chapter highlights aspects of a longer view of journalism which to an extent endorses this perspective. It lays great store in the vitality and variety of journalism and stresses the fact that it is best appreciated by broadening our concept of what constitutes journalism. This is achieved by studying the full range of product from tabloid and celebrity culture to magazines and television bulletins. Such studies help us to quantify the extent to which journalism is merely shifting to accommodate contemporary tastes and the extent to which it can be demonstrated that it is in fact departing from socially and politically important functions. Education is one of the ways of reflecting upon what the product should be across a variety of media, how it is most effectively and most ethically generated and to a large extent forces a consideration of how journalism can be distinguished from other forms of social communication in the contemporary technological era.

FURTHER READING

There is a vast literature on the product of journalism but the few titles here indicate the sort of range of inquiry touched upon, from radical explorations of what sort of journalism is produced under particular political conditions to the specific products of niche journalism especially popular at universities:

Altheide (2010) *Terror Post 9/11 and the Media*, Peter Lang. This explores the sort of journalism which started to emerge after 9/11 and 7/7. It explores the narratives and counter-narratives which we have come to expect as the normal frames of reference for our news in the new reporting paradigm.

Berkowitz (2010) *Cultural Meanings of News*, Sage. This explores some of the main questions associated with the product of news within its cultural context. What is news? How is it continuing to maintain its position and authority within social and political contexts? How does it function as a narrative, a communal activity and as an aid to cultural memory?

Davies (2008) *Flat Earth News*, Chatto and Windus, is a lament for the declining traditions of independent investigative journalism.

Keeble, Tulloch and Zollman (2010) *Peace Journalism: War and conflict resolution*, Peter Lang. This benefits from a foreword from eminent investigative journalist John Pilger and critiques mainstream journalism from a range of geo-political contexts such as the

UK, USA, Germany, Pakistan and the Philippines. It brings together journalists, theorists and campaigners in a provocative discussion of how journalism can be made into a tool for change and in the promotion and maintenance of peace.

Lloyd (2004) *What the Media are Doing to Our Politics*, Constable. This is a polemic response to what the author perceives as the dangerous influence of a sceptical news media on the political process.

Stephenson and Bromley (1998) *Sex, Lies and Democracy*, Longman, is an early exploration of the implications of a reliance on sensation to fuel the news media.

As Journalism Studies develops its range of courses and channels of enquiry, niche areas are constantly being developed. This is nowhere more evident than in the growth of specific degree courses, for instance, Sports Reporting:

Fuller (2008) *Sportscasters/Sportscasting*, Routledge.

Gratton and Solberg (2007) *The Economics of Sports Broadcasting*, Routledge.

Steen (2007) *Sports Journalism: A multimedia primer*, Routledge.

6

JOURNALISM ACROSS BORDERS
IMPERIAL, INTERNATIONAL, GLOBAL

INTRODUCTION

Once upon a time all news was international news. It was a direct
consequence of expanding trade routes and improved transport
technologies in the early modern period. At home, within the
Western nation states which had developed a commercial print culture from the sixteenth century, news was strictly controlled, as it
might have led to unwelcome attention for ruling elites. News from
foreign parts was preferable to printers simply because it was safer.
Even as this situation changed and state controls on domestic news,
particularly political news, became untenable or undesirable, foreign
news continued to form an important part of the available information
diet. However, despite the ever present international dimension, for
most of journalism's history, studies of journalism have remained
securely within their own national territories and have therefore
lacked much in the way of international comparative perspective.
From this insider perspective, British journalism was routinely
assessed as a facilitator of imperial communication and power.

MOVING BEYOND NATIONAL ACCOUNTS

The routine accounts of overseas journalism were either personal
biographies, particularly of the heroic variety from foreign

correspondents, were limited to inclusion of colonial journalism into mainstream histories or consisted of accounts of the international telegraphy services such as Reuters. Little attention was paid to the specifics or singularities of journalism outside Britain from any critical perspective. This started to change under a dual impetus. First, the colonial territories began to provide their own accounts, particular of the deficiencies of a model of reporting which had become too transparently Western for their tastes. One trigger for this response was the setting up of training schemes for countries in the developing world, based on the dominant norms of the country involved in the training, whether this was the USA, the UK or the Soviet Union, from the 1950s to the 1980s as part of the dynamics of the Cold War. The second impetus came out of the influence of sociological studies of news in the UK. Golding (1977) provided an early account of the ways in which the professional norms of the developed world had been imposed upon colonial territories and what the implications of this were. Smith produced a fine early example of the international scope of journalism in 1979 which traced the parallel development of journalism in different geographical and political contexts over a period of 400 years.

IMPACT OF EMPIRE

In addition to these developments, the experience of empire had a flowback effect on perceptions of both Britain's role in the world and its influence on the subjugated territories and their peoples. Journalism was a key and subtle force in shaping both of these sets of opinion and to an extent it still has a residual effect on the self-image of the British in the world. MacKenzie (1986) has written broadly on the impact of imperialism on home audiences through popular media and this fits into wider explorations of the impact on Western Europeans in general (Pieterse, 1995) ensuring an understanding that such cultural readings are not simply adjacent to national identities in the West but an essential ingredient, historically woven within them. Kiernan (1969) had already explored the powerful messages of cultural superiority which the press, among other forms of communication, had managed to inculcate with broader British society in the heyday of empire in the late nineteenth and early twentieth centuries. These became so engrained in the practices and structures of reporting on the world beyond Britain that it is difficult to overemphasize the positional superiority implicit in the presentation of overseas news which imperialism has established. The fact that Elliott and Golding (1973) could identify recurring themes about moral and cultural inferiority across most of the coverage of the 'Third World' in Western news media comes as little surprise in this longer historical and political context.

The story is still narrated, seemingly from an objective professional perspective, but within frames which adhere tacitly to the historical realities of the imperial legacy. Nor is it confined to the past. Gerbner and Marvanyi (1983) explored a week's worth of foreign coverage from the early 1970s and demonstrated what one might have suspected: that Western Europe and North America, and their associated interests, provided the bulk of the subject matter of international news. Sreberny-Mohammadi (1984) drew the same conclusions as part of a UNESCO-sponsored study. Heather Jean Brookes (1995) provides a thorough analysis of how cultural frames determine the reporting of Africa in the British elite press in the provocatively entitled research paper 'Suit, Tie and a Touch of Ju-Ju', published in *Discourse and Society*. Seasoned African correspondent John Ryle (1997) complemented this approach by his own observations drawn from decades of reporting from Africa when he claimed in the *Guardian* that it is no surprise that Western news media get Africa wrong since they do not understand the history or politics of the continent and do not have journalists trained in the languages spoken there. This ignorance limits both the levels of comprehension and the range of contributors, since journalists are restricted to talking to those who speak English and only therefore have access to a limited range of local reference.

BRITISH JOURNALISM AND EUROPE

There are powerful cultural explanations for the lack of understanding of foreign affairs within Britain's news media in general. Anderson and Weymouth (1999) have scrutinized the routinely anti-European slant of much of the highly influential newspaper coverage of Britain's relationship with the EU. This has been taken as indicative of what amounts to an identity crisis affecting the UK in the contemporary world as reflected through its journalism. Britain has lost its imperial power, but not the cultural assumptions about its own place in the world and the associated reflex to denigrate the world beyond its shores and imagine cooperation with its closest geographical neighbours as a consistent threat to British sovereignty.

CONTEMPORARY HISTORICAL APPROACHES

More recently, it has been within the realms of the global and international that serious history has begun to engage with the products of journalism, and with the interconnections of journalism with the political economy of imperialism. This trend allows a broadening out of Journalism Studies into a wider scope of study as international scholars begin to analyse the differences and similarities within traditions of journalism in various geo-political settings.

For many, journalism is an Anglo-American construct. The failure of the Soviet-sponsored political and economic systems of governance has been explained partially as demonstrating the inability of an authoritarian model to deal with the information flow which forms the lifeblood of Western liberal models of journalism. America is an essential exemplar of these Western traditions and Schudson (2008) would go further in claiming it as a specifically American phenomenon at source. Whether or not this is true, journalism has acted as an invaluable historical comparison in relations between the USA and the UK. Much scholarship has centred on this dynamic (Wiener, 1988; Wiener and Hampton, 2007). A more critical perspective on the American dominance of the news media comes in the thesis that the USA has exploited its position as the primary definer of journalism practice to create a system of global media imperialism (Boyd-Barrett, 1977c; Hallin, 1994; Tunstall and Machin, 1999).

However, since the breakup of the empires and colonies of the nineteenth and early twentieth centuries and the more recent decline of the political influence of the Soviet Union on its region and its client states, it has become apparent that some of the norms of the Anglo-American model of journalism no longer fit the realities of the world today. The lack of a global enemy has meant that the Western media claims to independence and impartiality can no longer be asserted against an opposing system of authoritarian control. On the contrary, they need now to be assessed with a harsh spotlight on their own merits and performance. This is a much more demanding task. Expectations of audiences at home have also changed. What do concepts such as 'objectivity' and 'balance' really mean when covering complex events overseas for a heterogeneous audience at 'home'? How should news of the Islamic world be relayed to countries with substantial Muslim populations? Increased flows of migrants have meant that it has become ever more difficult to provide the sort of distanced reporting that had become associated with the easier narratives of imperial identities (Seib, 2002).

COUNTER-NARRATIVES

Since the breakdown of the older imperial models of global hegemony, journalism has come to be seen in the context of a diverse, post-colonial set of traditions. In contradiction to liberal accounts of journalism as a force deployed on behalf of political freedom and against the interests of the powerful, historical accounts have begun to highlight the role of journalism as a colonial product and as a weapon used for purposes of subjugation. Journalism Studies is the meeting point for many of the debates emerging from within and outside Anglo-American critical traditions of scholarship. Historically, accounts begin with studies of the role of the colonial press in North America (Sloan and Williams, 1994), but they also span Britain's role in Ireland and the broader swathes of the British Empire. Here, historians have used studies of journalism as a critical/comparative tool to explore the role of communication within the structures of power exercised across geographically dispersed peoples (Potter, 2005). Journalism has also been studied as a means of exploring the sorts of stereotype construction necessary for the subjugation of colonial peoples such as the Irish (de Nie, 2004).

Journalism Studies has become a nexus of interconnections and from a British-based perspective explores how journalism from the UK has combined and differed from traditions in the USA, Western Europe, Australia, South Africa, the Indian subcontinent and Ireland to place Britain in a whole set of relationships with other global variants of journalism. Sparks and Tulloch (2000) add an unusual but much needed gloss in their international comparisons between differing styles of a global tabloid culture.

JOURNALISM AS A GLOBAL PRACTICE

From a historical perspective, it is clear that journalism, starting off from studies of imperial politics and acknowledging the fact of journalism's rapid spread around the world, needs a comparative international framework for study if we are to fully grasp its power and its promise. We have recently seen concerted attempts to draw on the observations of historians within the contemporary world and to go beyond the passive acceptance of Western predominance and influence – in short, attempts to de-Westernize studies of journalism in the world today. The Anglo-American model is challenged by a wave of writers from within and outside the Anglo-American sphere, with Curran and Park (2000) setting up a polemical position challenging the easy hegemony of traditional Western models of production and interpretation.

Siebert's (1965) model of the four theories of the press has remained remarkably resilient to the changing realities of the world of news media. The first is the Authoritarian theory, where an enlightened elite determine the flow of information; the second is the Libertarian theory, which maximizes the individual's right to seek out and explore information; the third is that of Social Responsibility, which proposes the duties of concerned public communicators; the fourth is the Soviet Communist theory, which is in effect an expanded state-driven version of the old Authoritarian theory. It was only recently that alternative grand narratives have been attempted to supplant it, such as Hallin and Mancini's (2004) highly influential account of the variants within globalized journalism practice today on a cultural-political spectrum. This was a much-needed updating of former attempts to systematize comparative models of journalism around the word.

Voltmer (2011) tries to expand our currently limited engagement with the concept of news and the public sphere which has been cocooned for too long within Western and, even more narrowly, Western European constrictions. She provides a more inter-nationalized account of the continuities as well as the differences in approaches to the role of news within public space. Hackett and

Zhao (2005) had already highlighted this diversity in their study, which draws upon the variety of political struggles across the globe to demonstrate that not only is the concept of democracy a less than universally accepted aspiration but that, in media terms, reaching the levels of participation in public life which is demanded by different peoples in differing circumstances is far from a uniform set of expectations. Both democracy and the role of the news media in the democratic process mean different things for different cultures. Each state has its own particular set of circumstances under which people struggle to wrestle information from politicians, who in their own interests seek to retain control of the levers of power. Within the ethics of journalism, there is an increasing awareness that one size does not fit all. Work by Ward and Wasserman (2010) demonstrates the range of differing understandings of journalism ethics across geo-political spaces and yet the view remains that it is as much in the respect for different traditions as in the search for common goals, that success and indeed solidarity for journalists may lie. Of particular note is the emergence of China as an area of burgeoning scholarship and academic scrutiny. This work is appreciative of China's own historical traditions of public communication, its engagement with colonial influences from East and West and how its contemporary journalism fits within the contrasting demands of these contours, in addition to more global paradigms, as it seeks to develop its own negotiation with state control of journalism.

PUBLISHING BEYOND THE NATIONAL

Good academic publishing should by definition be of relevance to an international audience of scholars. Publishing which touches upon journalism certainly reaches that goal. Individual ventures and broad publishing strategies have pursued this agenda, leading to an increase in international comparisons from a British base and a general enrichment of our understanding of the diversity and parallelism within journalism's global practices. More established social science media journals such as *Media, Culture and Society* and the *European Journal of Communication* have played an important role in providing analytical and historical accounts of journalism outside Britain. These publications enable contemporary aspects of journalism to be appreciated within the historical specificity of each of journalism's cultures. The journal *Media History* has been highly influential in developing these studies. Starting as a periodical pamphlet in 1984, it was adopted by American publisher Greenwood in 1991 and produced as an annual hardback research monograph 1994–96 before moving to eventual publication with Taylor & Francis.

The launch in 2000 of *Journalism Studies* and *Journalism: Theory, Practice and Criticism* heralded a new level of concentration on research into journalism on a global scale. These journals enabled comparative work from across the world to be considered by a truly international audience, and regular special editions with focus ranging from journalism and the European Union, and journalism in Latin America, to the role of foreign correspondents, draw upon a wide section of national perspectives. The success of these journals has contributed to the establishment of special journalism divisions at globally oriented research conferences, such as the International Communications Association (ICA), European Communication Research and Education Association (ECREA) and International Association of Media and Cultural Research (IAMCR), further enhancing the reputation of the subject area.

GLOBALIZATION

One of the key terms in current debates where the practice of journalism confronts the social and cultural commentaries on the world that journalism communicates is 'globalization'. The concept of globalization has received a great deal of critical attention over the past twenty years. It has two faces. The first presents itself as a levelling force, bringing similarities and eroding cultural, linguistic and social differences. The second flows from the greater familiarity with other cultures which comes from the increase in global trade and travel. This is manifested in a rejection of the process of homogenization, a rejection of foreign influences and a desire to reinforce more local traditions (Barber, 1995). One view is therefore that it constitutes a homogenizing force. The other is that it elicits a differentiation as a reaction against the perceived threat of increasing conformity. Featherstone (1993) provides a longer view of the process of globalization which takes us back to the dawn of modern capital organization and argues that we are witnessing merely the latest chapter in one of the key dynamics of modernity.

Just as printing from the mid-fifteenth century was key to the birth of journalism, the voyages of discovery of that century opened up the economic links which ushered in the first stages of the global era. These consolidated the economic exchanges first encouraged by the silk and spice routes. Communication and capital flowed along the same routes and the one reinforced the other. In fact, it is true to say that in many ways communication became a form of capital both in itself and in the lubrication of trade. Beyond this, at the high point of imperialism, reporting on international affairs became mapped, quite literally, onto the contours of the eighteenth- and nineteenth-century European empires. The invention of the telegraph reinforced the structure and flow of these communication patterns from the 1860s. Kaul (2003), for one, has explored the links between the British-based Reuters news agency and the political elite in the British Empire in India. In addition to considerations of political power, news from home was a key component in maintaining a sense of British community overseas (Harris, 1981). The structure of these imperial activities is still woven into many of the institutions and communicative assumptions of the twenty-first century, although not without dissenting voices. The process of globalization has reinforced the spread of Anglo-American norms of journalism around the world but has also prompted investigations of its inadequacies. An articulate polemic on the way in which global media are supplanting the rather more straightforward American media imperialism is contained in Herman and McChesney (1997), which presents the global media enterprises in quasi-religious terms, as missionaries for a particular brand of global capitalism. If journalism has always contained the seeds of capital within its practices, then, in this latest version of a globalized environment, they argue, it is acting as the disseminator of a new global belief system as a successor to older models of nationally based imperial dominance.

JOURNALISM STUDIES AND THE GLOBAL

There are two strands to Journalism Studies' engagement with the global. The first lies in studying how journalism has increasingly enabled researchers to appreciate the ways in which it has influenced history outside the boundaries of the dominant centres of journalism in the Anglo-American world. This has meant a finer understanding of the power relationships in the political world and the power of journalism as a political and cultural tool of oppression or enlightenment. The second strand explores how the practice of journalism has been influenced by technologies which enable the transmission and the ownership of news media on a wider global stage than ever before. This has led to the development of more comparative studies of what similarities and what differences exist between different national varieties of journalism, and the extent to which journalism's technological and corporate convergence is challenged by global alternatives such as Indymedia or more individualized engagements with online information. This also prompts the question of how the next generation of journalists are being prepared to deal with the complexities of globalized journalism; research into this question is producing interesting food for comparative thought. Cottle (2009), for one, believes that Journalism Studies is helping this transitional process.

GLOCAL

Responses to the perceived dominance of Anglo-American models have been varied. First, we have seen the emergence of more localized appreciations of the global drawing upon the reality that the news media are still consumed predominantly at a local/national level despite the potential for trans-border dissemination and collection. This should come as little surprise since the symbolic community which journalism has always structured is at a much lower level than the global. These apparent contradictions have given rise to the term 'glocalization' (Robertson, 1995). Second, we have seen attempts to shift the traditional priorities of journalism when dealing with international affairs rejecting bland cultural relativism. These have varied from development journalism (Kariithi, 1994) and peace journalism (Lynch and McGoldrick, 2005) to professional questioning of practices in the face of international conflicts (Bell, 1995, 1998).

GLOBAL JOURNALISM EDUCATION

As Journalism Studies becomes more formalized in higher education and within the academic research community, it has become easier to track comparisons and contrasts in how journalism is pursued and produced across the globe. One of the most interesting aspects of global journalism research is the way that it connects with imperial and colonial legacies and this, in turn, sheds light on the range of strategies which the cultures of journalism around the world have used to survive and even flourish in very different circumstances. This has enabled the subject area to begin an engagement with the geo-politics of its own history and the de-Westernizing trends in studies of the media in general. Interesting cross-cultural comparisons of journalism have been published, such as Zhu et al. (1997), Frölich and Holtz-Bacha (2003) and Hanna and Sanders (2007).

In order to consolidate these discussions of journalism education on a global level, a range of national organizations have come together in common cause to establish the World Journalism Education Congress, which was hosted in 2008 in Singapore and in 2010 in South Africa. It appears clear from the procedings of these gatherings that, within a broad-based understanding of what purposes and ideals journalism should aspire to, there exist different models and traditions as well as different ideas of how best to map an education onto these differing views of journalism across the globe.

In terms of educational provision for postgraduate research students, there is also the emergence at the University of Westminster of the study of journalism as part of general media system explorations in China, Africa and the Arabic-speaking world. Here, as well as at Cardiff, Leeds and Sheffield, there are flourishing graduate schools which encourage research into overseas journalism as part of their PhD programmes. This has enabled the subject area to further its engagement with the geo-politics of its own history and the de-Westernizing trends in studies of the media in general.

THE GLOBAL JOURNALIST

There was a time when comparisons conducted on the context and aspirations of journalists' roles tended to be national in orientation. Early examples were predominantly focused on the well-developed self-reflection of the American journalist, as exemplified by Johnston et al. (1976). What then are the features of journalism that can claim universality? Randall (1996) has provided a provocative and eloquent plea for general aspirations for all journalists in his book *The Universal Journalist*, but just how transferable and adaptable are journalism's core ideals and principles? Are the ideals of journalism such as 'objectivity' and 'freedom of expression' Western ideals or do they have regional variants which combine to form a globalized understanding of communicative ethics? Cross-cultural, cross-national research into the implications of a more globalized markets for journalism is taking place. Weaver (1998) provides an edited collection of a wide-ranging assessment of the diversity of approaches to the roles and expectations of journalists which continue to probe whether they constitute Western traditions as part of a media-colonization or whether they contain elements of universality which can be taught across cultures and differing political conditions.

CONCLUSION

International scholarship has enabled genuinely fresh insights into how journalism has operated beyond the national, both historically and in the contemporary world. It assists furthermore in assessing claims and counter-claims regarding the nature of the relationship between global and local cultures. Journalism may be geographically a global enterprise but it lacks much in the way of cultural global coherence. It may be opening up geo-political markets for large media conglomerates and thereby discussions of difference and similarity, but cultural convergence is nowhere in sight. Global exploration of comparative trends in shifts in news values, the power and influence of news media representations, the organization of journalism, the speed of adoption of new technologies of communication, the impact of politics: in all these areas global research encourages theoretical paradigms which can universalize and also refine specific areas of practice. Global comparative models have emerged out of this sort of sustained exploration, such as the groundbreaking Hallin and Mancini (2004). Global journalism research helps us to appreciate, at best, the micro- and the macro-levels of journalistic practice. Global products produced by increasingly global organizations with integrated hierarchies of production have been able to deploy new technologies to extend their reach, penetration and profitability. At the same time, Indymedia-style developments show how the same technology can be used to extend alternative views of the world to larger and more diffuse audiences to great political effect.

FURTHER READING

Allan and Thorsen (2009) *Citizen Journalism: Global perspectives*, Peter Lang. This draws upon practice from a wide range of geopolitically diverse countries such as Brazil, China, India, Iran, Iraq, Kenya and Vietnam.

Anderson and Ward (2006) *The Future of Journalism in the Advanced Democracies*, Ashgate. The authors of this book have long been concerned with the role of journalism in the democratic process. Here they take a wide view of contemporary developments.

Deuze (2002) 'National News Cultures: Towards a profile of journalists using cross-national survey findings'. *Journalism and Mass Communication Quarterly* 79 (1): 134–49.

McNair (2006) *Cultural Chaos: Journalism and power in a globalised world*, Routledge. This is a radical and controversial reconceptualization of how journalism is actually functioning in the contemporary world. It aims to disturb complacent views of journalism and its cultural and political status.

Preston (2009) *Making the News: Journalism and news cultures in Europe*, Routledge, provides a rich European context to these discussions.

Ward and Wasserman (2010) *Media Ethics Beyond Borders: A global perspective*, Routledge, draws upon a wide range of international expertise to ponder the central question of the adaptability and transferability of ethical considerations across borders and cultures focussing predominantly on news media.

Weaver (1998) *The Global Journalist: News people around the world*. This started the ball rolling in many respects and is the generator of much excellent subsequent work as well as a fully reconsidered and updated approach in a new book co-edited with Willnat: Weaver and Willnat (2012) *The Global Journalist in the 21st Century*, which provides a comprehensive analysis of data from interviews and observation in thirty countries.

7

JOURNALISM STUDIES: ENGAGEMENTS WITH TECHNOLOGY AND INDUSTRIAL CHANGE

INTRODUCTION

Amidst the hurly-burly of contemporary technological innovations, it is easy to lose sight of the fact that technology brought journalism into existence and that journalism is very much defined by its continuing ability to react and adapt to changes in the technological environment. Gutenberg's experiments with adapting a wine press to hold moveable type and his testing of new recipes for suitable ink in fifteenth-century Mainz began a process which culminated in the development of regular periodical publications from the early seventeenth century. The journalism which these publications carried was to be affected by refinements and increased efficiencies which altered the shape, market and audience of journalism down three centuries before the new technology of radio forced a radical reconsideration of the traditions which print journalism had established. But it is easy to forget that, before this, print journalism had been radically restructured by the Industrial Revolution's development of steam printing, the emergence of the photograph and rotogravure printing, as well as through the impact on the form and content of the press of first the telegraph and then the telephone and the typewriter. Furthermore, it was very much the popular press which drove the incorporation of technological change as it sought more commercial success in introducing bigger headlines, more pictures and made better use of the efficiencies of railway distribution.

THE LIMITS OF TECHNOLOGY

Journalism needs to be studied with one eye on its ability to incorporate technological development so that we are not lured into any lazy assumptions that journalism is merely part of a process of constant improvement or, from the opposite perspective, one of terminal decline on account of the impact of technology. Technology, in isolation, has never made journalism better or worse. Views of this relationship between journalism and technology are located somewhere along a spectrum between technological determinism and symptomatic technology. The first, technological determinism, argues that social and economic events are driven by changes in technology. The second maintains the exact opposite: that it is social and economic changes which allow technology to be adopted on terms which are shaped by the existing cultural environment. Technology does not drive change. It has to adapt to the patterns of cultural expectation within particular societies at specific moments in time. An assessment of journalism and technology needs insight from both the practice of journalism as well as a general awareness of broader cultural trends and how technology forms part of social history. As social historians have turned their scrutiny to the technologies of journalism, it has become abundantly clear that the development and adoption of particular technologies by journalism are processes which have been shaped by political and economic factors which lie outside journalism itself and indeed outside of any absolute consideration of the quality of journalism's products.

HISTORY AND TECHNOLOGY

Historians of the Industrial Revolution have observed how *The Times* newspaper invested in its steam-driven printing presses from the German manufacturer König Bauer at a moment in 1816 that was so propitious that it was able to outstrip all other newspapers and build up a competitive advantage by gambling early financial outlay on an unproven technology in an uncertain political environment for newspapers. However, with regards to the next major techno-logical development, the telegraph, although telegraphic commu-nication had become the norm by the 1850s and transatlantic dispatches began from 1865, *The Times* by the end of the Franco-Prussian War in 1871 had allowed its serious rivals to steal a march on it in the deployment of this channel of communication. By the time that photography and telegraphy were staples on more popular newspapers in the early twentieth century, *The Times* was holding itself aloof from what were considered to be rather unworthy and cheap intrusions into the practices of what had become the elite people's newspaper of record. It was no longer willing to initiate risks on technologies which it did not consider within the orbit of the paper's image of itself. Illustration in general and photography in particular were avoided by most of the elite press until the twentieth century as they subscribed to the undeclared prejudice that pictures were for the common throng and that their clients wanted to maintain a highly literate engagement with their news-paper. Although by the 1880s there had been a perfectly acceptable way of reproducing half-tone photographs in newspapers, demon-strated by the *Daily Graphic*, *The Times* ignored this development until the outbreak of the First World War.

TELEGRAPHIC SENTENCES

One of the most spectacular mismatches between technology and the production of journalism came, in fact, with the telegraph. It has been anecdotally credited with the introduction of the 'tele-graphic sentence' and the 'inverted pyramid' of the newspaper. The telegraph was able to provide a regular supply of national and international news by the 1860s and it had become commonly accepted that the mode of delivery of information down the wire had led newspapers to concentrate their efforts on constructing a short introductory paragraph at the start of a news story which answered all the important questions: Who? What? Why? Where? When? How? The rest of the story continued in diminishing order of importance, meaning that editing on the basis of cost or space could be done from the bottom up without disturbing the impor-tant features at the start of the item. Time on the wires also cost money so there was a financial incentive to order the information as efficiently and as briefly as possible. The telegraphic sentence which was to become so much a part of Alfred Harmsworth's success on his various newspapers in the early twentieth century was certainly a consequence of the technology which gave it its name, yet more empirical approaches to the language of journalism which have flowed from Journalism Studies (Pöttker, 2003; Hoyer and Pöttker, 2005) indicate that the process was one driven not by the technology but at a pace dictated by the newspapers themselves. The inverted pyramid became a common feature of newspapers in Britain as late as the 1920s, over half a century after the first transatlantic cables were laid and fully seventy years after the commercial development of the telegraph in a European context. From the 1920s it became the only form of reporting style taught to journalists and soon afterwards the account of the influence of the telegraph in its development began to be presented as unchallenged wisdom despite the fact that the telegraph was incorporated much more slowly within the culture and economics of the newspaper.

RADIO MAKES WAVES

Radio was the first technological challenge to the omnipotence of print and it had an extraordinarily swift impact on the style and ambition of the press as a whole – an impact whose consequences we are arguably still living through today! The interesting thing about the technology of radio broadcasting was that, unlike the more established practices of newspaper journalism, radio emerged into a fully rounded, democratic culture of debate on the political implications of any new technology. This meant that we have evidence of the discussions and rationale which formed the establishment's conditions for allowing the medium to develop in the way it did. Radio was introduced with a mingling of fear of the potential impact of a truly mass medium and a political anxiety that it should be kept out of the hands of the powerful, whether the rich or the political elite, so as to prevent it from being turned into a form of propaganda. The way that the British government handled the introduction of radio broadcasting, and radio journalism in particular, therefore tells us much about radio as a social technology. From the start, there were revealing discussions of the nature of radio broadcasting, and government reports were commissioned on the most effective way of managing the introduction of radio into British society. The political environment for the emergence of radio broadcasting could not have been more demanding, as the Representation of People Act, passed in 1918, entitled all men and women over the age of thirty to full voting rights for the first time. The state was keen to see the new mass medium developed in such a way as to enhance the democratic potential of this Act of Parliament. The government-sponsored Sykes Report in 1923 was the most significant early record of these discussions and first articulated the vision of a public service broadcaster. The newly appointed Director General, John Reith, penned a seminal account with something approaching a missionary's zeal. *Broadcast over Britain* (1924) was his vision of the potential of radio in informing, educating and entertaining the nation.

Of course, the BBC has a mass of archival records of its deliberations, policy-making processes and strategies towards technological innovation across almost a century of journalism's history, but these have needed the professional historian and academic to open them up to a fully critical scrutiny. The work of Briggs (1961, 1965, 1970a, 1970b, 1995) and others has been supplemented by insightful memoirs which often go much further in analysing social and political contexts for the simple but significant reason that broadcast journalism in the UK, with its statutory public service brief, has always needed to be more reflexive than the purely profit-driven and archly pragmatic newspaper industry.

Despite the mass of documentation and the articulate reminiscences of former BBC employers and managers, it was not until social historians began to draw the huge wealth of archive material together that a more complete, dispassionate and accurate picture began to emerge. This started with Briggs and moved through Scannell and Cardiff's (1991) sadly unfinished project, all of which anchored the development of broadcasting within a solidly social environment, showing the ways in which decision-making was negotiated between political, public and increasingly commercial interests.

The rise of radio's reputation through the 1930s and especially through the war years was achieved because the BBC was able to demonstrate a genuine contribution to the maintenance of democratic communication at a time where mediated communication had become the plaything of totalitarian states in many parts of the world. On account of this growing global prestige for a homegrown news medium and because of the technical improvements which enabled the radio to broadcast more up-to-date information to greater numbers of people than a newspaper could do, the newspapers moved to adapt their own product to this challenge. The attempts to grab a larger share of the popular market was evident to the daily consumer of popular newspapers in the 1930s as competitions, price wars and the offers of free gifts, ranging from the complete works of Dickens to a free piano, all vied for the loyalty of subscribers as newspapers battled for audience share. Less noticeable was the shift, particularly in the popular press but one which would eventually come to impact upon all newspapers, to develop a more punning, less informational style of reporting: one with a more clearly marked appeal to the language and interests of their readers and more characterized by opinion than the radio journalism which had a commitment not to editorialize and to remain unmarked by party political preference. The trend for newspapers to articulate direct support for particular political positions on behalf of their readers was, in effect, consolidated by the obligation of radio journalism to provide a more literal and balanced account of the news.

TELEVISION JOURNALISM: CAUTIOUS FIRST STEPS

The same anxieties displayed towards radio journalism were also in evidence as television was slowly introduced into Britain after the end of the Second World War. Television in its early years at the BBC was restricted by fears emanating from the technology itself. The visual had always appeared to be more aligned with the entertainment industries, the music hall, the popular magazine and now the cinema. The BBC was worried that the lofty aims of the Corporation would be compromised by the intrusion of too much visuality into its journalism. The early offerings of television journalism on the BBC were characterized by attempts to restrain the impact of the visual onto the aural approach which it had perfected. Examples of this were a preference for the voice-over of footage, as had been the standard practice in Movietone newsreels from the

1920s and the less visual news being narrated off-screen, dis-embodied with a caption in front of the camera such as a picture of Big Ben or the Houses of Parliament. Newsreaders on-screen, which had been the norm in the USA for many years, were not countenanced as it was felt that such a display of personalization would have compromised the Corporation's carefully nurtured impression of impartiality. Little of this early output was recorded, so we have to depend on analysis of archival material and anecdotal accounts. Whale's *Eye Half Shut* (1969) and Wyndham Goldie (1977) were notable early examples. Social historians of the media and former BBC employees have made rich contributions to this strand of Journalism Studies. It plays an important role in relativiz-ing the impact of new technologies in journalism in the present as much as teaching us about the conditions of incorporation of technologies in the past.

THE CATALYST OF THE POPULAR

The leap towards a more positive engagement with television journalism came not through the introduction of any technology but rather from the spur to the BBC of a commercial competitor which needed to create a much more popular format in order to attract advertising based on its promise to provide large audiences. Culturally this sort of commercial television journalism drew much upon experiences of American broadcasting and included from the start a much more personality-led style of reporting, a less defer-ential attitude to politicians and an approach which sought to engage with a younger audience for television news than had hitherto been evident. Again, it was not the technology which created the decline in deference but a set of cultural and social shifts in attitudes to authority in general in the years following the Second World War which were able to break into public con-sciousness because of a political decision to allow commercial broadcasting to find more populist ways to compete with the more staid offerings of the traditionalist BBC. Television could in princi-ple point the camera at the warts and all, but only an editorial decision could include them, just as radio, particularly during the Second World War, had encouraged people to be more sceptical of what they read in the press. The way that this newly invigorated journalistic product was introduced required the press in turn to respond to a broader set of threats to its own products. Newspapers sought to align their coverage with the newly popular journalistic medium by themselves covering much of the celebrity culture generated by television and adding commentary and reviews on popular programmes. Newspapers shifted swiftly into the supplementary area of colour magazines, starting with the *Sunday Times* in 1962, and dropped the last vestiges of anonymity for their own journalists. The reason for this was simple. There was no point in retaining the anonymity of journalists when television journalists were becoming household names and celebrities in their own right! The by-line and, increasingly, an accompanying photograph started to appear on a regular basis. Recognizing that the provision of the latest news with pictures could no longer be the exclusive preserve of the newspaper, the press in Britain attempted to move one step ahead of its broadcast rivals and ushered in the great decade of serious investigative reporting, from the *Sunday Times* Insight Team from 1963 at the elite end of the market to 'Mirrorscope' and 'Shock Issues' in the popular tabloid the *Daily Mirror*.

By the early 1960s, the majority of the British public were using television news as their main source of information and continuing research from the Mass Observation Unit provided regular examples of the public's views and uses of their news media products. The confidence that this engendered provided managers and owners with good reason to invest in more and more technological wizardry to enhance the instantaneous nature of their product. This economically driven investment meant that satellite technology quickly enabled foreign news to be reported more efficiently, first from the launch of Telstar in 1962 but more completely from the coverage of the Yom Kippur War in 1973. At the same time as these technological enhancements flowed from the commercial success of television journalism, the newspapers continued in their pursuit of a more opinionated engagement with the lifestyle of their increasingly affluent readers and they were able to make vast profits from demonstrating this appeal to advertisers. In fact, the newspapers' expression of candid opinion enabled them to emphasize the political and social differentiation of their conduct even more, while the statutory restrictions of editorializing meant that the television remained restrained in comparison and appeared to be directed at a more homogeneous set of audiences at both national and regional levels.

TELEVISION: THE GREAT ENTERTAINER

There remains the question of just how appropriate television is as a medium for journalism. Some argued from the early years that, as an entertainment-based medium, television was incapable of producing the sort of rational, in-depth discussion found in the best of the newspapers. This was exacerbated by the emergence of television out of the traditions of fictional film-making. Television journalism, aimed as it is at the general audience, is characterized by a single pace of delivery, a structure and presentational style which aim for ease of comprehension and a preference for issues which can be captured in an abbreviated sound-bite. Television news does not do complexity well. The concept of television as entertainment is addressed polemically in Postman (1986) and more recently in Thussu (2008). Proof of this tendency can be seen in the slide of television journalists in particular into prominent roles in entertainment programming. This is particularly prevalent at the BBC, where cross-pollination between news and other entertainment genres is more viable than in the commercial sector. Celebrity journalists are now being used as a subtle form of cross-promotion, exploiting the brand of the famous presenter to add consumer appeal to another programme beyond their usual journalistic patch. The problem for the BBC is that in increasing the visibility of their celebrity journalists, they are also inflating the journalists' expectations of larger salary packages, which in certain high-profile cases is now leading to a showdown with a government which sees excessive pay as an abuse of public money. Recent examples of such crossovers include Andrew Marr (*Darwin's Dangerous Idea*; *The Making of Modern Britain*), Jeremy Paxman (*University Challenge*; *Spelling*), Fiona Bruce (*Police, Camera, Action*; *Antiques Roadshow*), David Dimbleby (*Seven Ages of Britain*) and John Humphrys (*Mastermind*), and there always seems to be at least one BBC presenter featured in *Strictly Come Dancing* (Christine Bleakley, Chris Hollins). The celebrification of journalists acts as a guarantor of audience ratings – journalists as the ultimate news media brands. It has drawn attention from both academic commentators and fellow journalists writing as columnists in newspapers.

TECHNOLOGY AND POLITICAL/ECONOMIC ENVIRONMENT

Historical accounts of journalism have also highlighted how technology has lagged behind economic and political trends in determining the shape of newspapers at the end of the twentieth century. The restructuring of an industry which was by any objective assessment antiquated by the end of the Second World War was to be further delayed, not by the unavailability of new ways of doing things, but by the opposition of a very well-organized workforce to any changes to their traditional work patterns. Restrictions on paper supply had continued after the rationing of the war but this had the paradoxical affect of keeping printing costs low and advertising space expensive. This meant that if the print unions were in no hurry to change their ways, the owners also had no need to divert their energies into any confrontation or into any real engagement in new technology. By the early 1970s there was the facility for journalists to input their own copy and it had been experimented with on the *Nottingham Evening Post*. However, there was no corresponding economic imperative to introduce it and no political framework which would allow the owners to ride rough-shod over the working practices of their printers or their journalists. This was all to change in the 1980s as, under the strongly anti-trade union Conservative government of Margaret Thatcher, legislation combined with the economic ambition of one particular newspaper owner to change the newspaper world forever.

The technological changes introduced at the new purpose-built plant in the old East End of London by Rupert Murdoch at Wapping in 1986 were significant in that they allowed journalists to directly input copy onto computer screens while sub-editors and page editors could then manipulate the content on screen. However, these changes were not as significant as the economic and political factors which accompanied their introduction. All printers working for Murdoch's News Corporation and producing *The Times*, the *Sunday Times*, the *News of the World* and the *Sun* were summarily sacked as the organization moved literally overnight to the Wapping production plant. Computer-based typesetting replaced the now redundant skills of the linotype printers. This meant that increases in pagination, the use of colour and the insertion of supplements with their additional advertising, up to the last minute in the production process, all heralded an economic boom for newspaper owners, shelving staff at the same time as they tightened their grip on the remaining journalists, severed from their traditional union loyalties. Although this technology had been available for several years, its introduction had to wait for a compatible political climate such as that provided by the 1984 Trade Union Act, which restricted picketing to one's own place of work, limited the number of pickets allowed at any one time and prohibited solidarity secondary action. None of the printers were legally entitled to strike because Murdoch had set up Wapping as a separate company and so any picketing by his erstwhile staff would have been illegal. The plant was set up as a high-security stronghold and police enthusiastically interpreted the new anti-trade union legislation. Distribution of the plant's newspapers was effected by an Australian road haulage company TNT, so as to avoid the potential of any solidarity action from railway unions. Within a year all significant newspaper production in the capital had shifted to the new economically streamlined, technologically enhanced and massively more profitable computerized mode of production, as there was no other competitive solution to Murdoch's coup.

These events have been well chronicled by those who lived through them and by those who were affected by them as well as by analysts who have reflected upon the broader implications of their impact on journalism and its production (National Council for Civil Liberties, 1986; Wintour, 1989; MacArthur, 1988). Such accounts have contributed to a sustained critique of the social and political impact of technological changes introduced during this period as a significant experiment in the economics of the news media in Britain.

UTOPIA POSTPONED

Optimistic predictions of the potential of technological innovations at the time assumed that, beyond the economic pragmatism of

Murdoch, computer-based typesetting would enable smaller-scale desktop production and lead quickly to cheaper and more diverse news media environment. The reason this did not occur would be a mystery without a clear understanding of how journalism functions within a specific political economy. Established newspaper groups employed cross-ownership of chains of media products, hostile pricing strategies and colonized any and every broadly popular niche market as ways to prevent competitors launching smaller and more radical start-ups. Technology helped build profits and profits led to a more intensively corporatized journalism environment in which, for instance, investigative journalism, which takes a long time to research and a lot of investment to resource, became quickly relegated as secondary in importance to maintaining brand identity and profitability.

Studies of journalists in news media organizations demonstrate unequivocally that technology has been used as a way of increasing productivity and output with fewer journalists doing more writing based on less and less primary research. Journalists are more likely to be composing stories sitting at desks rather than exploring the world outside the walls of their organization. They have the equipment but they don't have the time to take it out of the office! Multi-skilling even at the BBC has led to a split in perceptions between managers, who want to drive down costs of production, with journalists working across traditional divides with equipment which would appear to enable them to do this, repurposing and recrafting their product for various delivery channels. On the other hand, journalists themselves would prefer to be allowed to use the new technology to produce a better product of improved quality, but they have less time and editorial space to effect this ambition.

QUANTITY NOT QUALITY

The momentum first generated by News Corporation's introduction of news technologies has continued through a period where technological innovation has been shaped by an environment where neo-liberal solutions to questions of information access have provided consumer-led rather than quality-led approaches to news production. The multiplication of delivery channels for journalism has not been accompanied by any tangible improvement in the quality or the range of news or comment provided. Rather, the opposite is true. In order to generate the sort of profits acceptable to global conglomerates, new technological investments have been deployed to produce quicker, cheaper and more marketable products. Broadcasting Acts in 1990 and 1996 consolidated the shift to a much more market-oriented approach to the provision of broadcast journalism. Empirical studies based on observations of news production practices by scholars and concerned journalists have been facilitated by the increased respectability and visibility of studies of journalism. This is nowhere better demonstrated that in the recent crossover study by Nick Davies (2008), published as *Flat Earth News*, which drew upon funded research by the School of Journalism Media and Communications at Cardiff University. His findings are echoed in another exemplary piece of research that explores the sourcing of news stories in the local press (O'Neill and O'Connor, 2008) and which discovered a similar situation where much material was being included without a proper investigation of accounts emerging from public relations outlets because of pressure on the time of journalists. This work on the relationships between the local press and their sources and the increasing reliance of local news media on publicity material is a milestone in this sort of enquiry, which demonstrates that the technologies are not necessarily being put to best use if the overarching drive is to make savings and get fewer journalists to do more work while keeping profit margins high. Franklin and Carlson (2011) have extended explorations of the relationships between journalists and sources within the changing technological landscape. Imagine that no such empirical studies were undertaken; we would be left with a few uncoordinated assessments and very probably the soothing sound of media managers and a few tame journalists assuring the public that all is in good hands and that profitability is forever driving up standards. One recalls the assertion by James Murdoch at the Edinburgh International Television Festival in 2009, in his attack on the BBC, that profit is the only guarantor of independence. As an antidote to such simplification, Journalism Studies has become an increasingly important voice in assessing the true impact of technology on the quality of journalism in the present and in demonstrating its highly uneven influence in the past.

QUESTIONS OF QUALITY

Journalists themselves have noted the ways in which the increased use of ever more sophisticated technologies has had a negative effect on the quality of news. Journalist and academic partnership Hargreaves and Thomas (2002) highlighted many issues affecting television's engagement with new technologies in their book *New News, Old News*, which was partially funded by the Independent Television Commission. The pressures generated by twenty-four-hour news or the use of live reporting from pre-selected locations do not necessarily enhance understanding. Cushion and Lewis (2010) have explored 'rolling news', this latest technological variant of the 'latest', and have compiled significant evidence that it purveys less analysis and more speculation than the conventional half-hour bulletins while relying – rather surprisingly, perhaps – on fewer reporters on location and fewer eye-witness accounts than one might expect. Instead it tends to recycle the agenda of the day and repeat minimally adjusted updates as well as announcements of what is to come. It brings us into the territory that French sociologist Bourdieu (1998) warned about: that of 'permanent amnesia'. For all this it has had an effect across the range of television, with all major providers rushing to provide what is perceived to be a vital market leader.

Advances in satellite and digital technologies, combined with the development of lightweight recording and transmission equipment, can bring striking live images where traditional cameras would have proved too cumbersome. The political realities of working alongside the Armed Forces on active duty in war zones means that, whatever the technological possibilities, journalism is restricted by the constraints of considerations which are more strategic than technological. Despite the potential for instant and constant availability of information, news from the battlefield is in many respects (Cottle, 2006; Matheson and Allan, 2009) more constrained than it was at the time of W.H. Russell's dispatches for *The Times* from the Crimean War. These had such an impact on political and social opinion back in Britain that it is claimed they prompted Florence Nightingale to travel to the war front to help with the wounded soldiers. The practice of 'embedding' journalists (Tumber and Palmer, 2004), despite its advantages in terms of safety and access, also creates a professional and cultural dilemma for the journalists in their attempts to remain objective.

DIGITAL DIVIDENDS?

Trust? Ethics? What distinguishes journalism from mere 'content'? From the mid-1990s, the internet and a whole new vocabulary of blogs, tweets, citizen journalists, user-generated content, news aggregators and wikis have stretched and challenged the boundaries of journalism. We have witnessed the rise of accounts of the impact of technology on social communication, including journalism, as the 'network society' (Castells, 1996). Some go further and see the combination of technological and cultural factors as inexorably leading to the death of journalism (Bromley, 1997). Within this changing environment, the nature of journalism and the composition of the public for which it is designed are also becoming more complex and difficult to define as they become more diffuse under the influence of technology's social incorporation. The audience is also being engaged with much more, in attempts to revitalize public engagement and, some argue, to drive down the costs of providing news, especially at a local level (Örnebring, 2008; Singer, 2009).

The most fascinating aspect of the latest, digitally driven techno-logical shifts in journalism is that they are occurring within a growing field of critical enquiry. When this is added to the imme-diacy brought about by the technology, there is a genuine impres-sion of informed research and debate emerging at the same time as the technologies are being integrated within news media practices. There are plenty of avenues for the dissemination of this reflection, as we have seen, and this peer-reviewed, published research is undoubtedly having an effect on the interpretation of technological change as it happens. Research into the impact of technology on the products of journalism has a triple effect: first, it helps dampen unrealistic enthusiasms; second, it curbs the technophilia tradition-ally emanating from the earliest assessments of media technologies (Innis, 1951: McLuhan, 1964); third, it leavens unmitigated gloom among seasoned professionals. Research also adds a valuable historical and empirical perspective to the debate. The appointment of a Johnston Press Chair of Digital Journalism at UCLAN in 2005–9 was an example of sustained and targeted enquiry into the implications of new technologies for journalism's political economy. Much work is also under way on the impact of new technologies on the practices of local and national newsrooms and in particular the ways in which the much-feted user-generated content continues to be moulded very much within the constraints of conventional editorial decision-making (Hermida and Thurmin, 2008; Hermida, 2010; Harrison, 2010). Niblock and Machin (2007) provided a contemporary account of the processes of newsgathering in a changing environment, and the same authors (Niblock and Machin, 2008) have also provided some very perceptive observations on the rebranding of the *Liverpool Echo*. All these research projects draw upon the blend of social science and humanities research methods established within Journalism Studies and which have evolved over the previous half-century.

The development of technologies such as lightweight digital cameras, smart mobile phones and portable computers have had a two-way influence on journalism. On the one hand, it is feasible for anyone in possession of such technologies who happens to be at the site of an occurrence which fits the news values of particular news organizations to provide a report which can be relayed to a worldwide audience online. On the other hand, professional, institutional journalism is under pressure to match the speed and immediacy of such coverage itself. These two pressures set up a contest between the claims of amateurism and professionalism. Let us characterize them as the 'blogger' and the 'journalist'. The blogger certainly has a raw and uncensored energy, but are the reports filed by a blogger authoritative and factual, and do they conform to acceptable standards of ethical and legal behaviour? The journalist is certainly working within the legal and ethical constraints which make his/her news organization confident that its reputation and bank balance will not be adversely affected by some scurrilous outburst or uncorroborated claims particularly directed towards wealthy celebrities with a penchant for defending their reputations in the courts. In addition, it is claimed that much blogging, no matter how edgy it appears, routinely ignores anything other than mainstream sources, and the majority of trusted blogging sources are actually journalists. The ultimate impact of these portable technologies, in combination with the all-pervasive internet, is in the pressure on journalism to provide as immediate a response to any event anywhere which limits the ability of longer-term investigations paid for out of a shrinking budget for journalism at the same time as it generates an increased expectation of speed of delivery where speed is in danger of becoming the ultimate aim of journalism. Audiences for journalism are increasingly being provided with accounts of the world which are presented within already restricted frames of reference and which routinely fail to do the difficult and controversial work of providing historical and political context. Journalism produced using these new technologies encourages us to inhabit a world of the constant present. The visual presentation of online converged news products give the impression of an environment where e-mails, texts, blogs and user-generated content provide a much more participatory engagement with news media audiences. However, such practices continue to be as editorially constrained and corporately driven as their old technology predecessors, the letters pages of newspapers and magazines. Contrary to the enthusiasms of the advocates of the new digital technologies, there has been no technologically driven democratic takeover of the news media. Fenton (2010) and others sceptically explore the possibilities of new technology as a springboard to new democratic engagement through the medium of journalism.

The narrowing of mainstream practices which new online technologies encourage in the current political economy of the news media is, however, moderated by the increasing availability of news archives, online repositories of journalists' columns and hyperlinks from online journalism into a richer selection of material for the amateur or professional researcher wanting more background to a particular story. This is a backroom development rather than something which is affecting the frontline of contemporary journalism, but it is a technological moment of progress for a more contextualized mode of information. One can only hope that ultimately its richness will expose the threadbare nature of the wall-to-wall twenty-four-hour journalism product. Ultimately, journalism will survive if its sources are authoritative, its content is accurate, its writing is engaging to specific audiences and, above all, if it can maintain a distance between the economic interests of its owners and the desire for its audiences to discover more about their world. This will remain the territory within which effective journalism continues to operate.

The development of journalism has always demonstrated an ability to select aspects of technological developments which fit within its core claims and the social expectations of what it provides to the public. Histories of technology and journalism demonstrate that an additive process characterizes journalism and that one technology has never simply disappeared because of the arrival of a newer one. However, journalism today is at a startling new point of its history. It is entirely possible that the new technologies flooding the practice of journalism may erode the very professional claims and social expectations of what journalism has until now provided as a distinctive contribution to our democratic forms of communication.

TECHNOLOGY AND EDUCATION

Technology leads to the temptation to believe that everyone, everywhere, is a journalist as the practice takes on a technologized global potential. This forces us to reconsider how journalism should be taught as it shifts quantitatively, with its digital archives, and online sources, and qualitatively, as boundaries with other communication media are thinned or become entirely porous. If social, technological, political and professional changes have all combined to force journalism and journalists to become more fluid in moving between shifting boundaries which demarcate their field of operation in increasingly unstable ways, how is this new reality addressed in journalism courses? Both Journalism Studies and education for journalism tend to privilege mainstream practices over alternatives which may disadvantage students emerging into the world of work as unable to deal with practices outside the traditional canon. Yet, in the contemporary journalism classroom, students are often adding themselves to current expertise as digital natives combine fortuitously with journalism's procedures and traditions.

Institutional practices shape product and practice and universities are responding quickly and reflectively to changing demands on the skills and competence of their graduates. Beyond the technology, journalism and its study remain an important area for civic engagement and especially at a time when its core values appear to be threatened by political and economic changes which have technologies at their back and which are being deployed to affect the results desired by industries driven by profit alone. This means that more than ever we need robust studies of what journalism means and how it operates and a solid educational framework for both future practitioners, active citizens and media-literate consumers (Pavlik, 2005).

CONCLUSION

To a large extent journalism has always been a tale of the engagements between technology and communication. The survival of journalism has depended on its successful navigation and then exploitation of the various challenges and opportunities of emerging technologies. Profit and impact. There are narratives and anxieties of the decline of journalism, or new dawns for it which resonate throughout history. Take, for example, the fear of the propaganda potential of radio technology and current debates about the personal power of Rupert Murdoch or the threat/utopian possibilities of the web. We've had them all before in various shapes and contexts. Winston (1998) – a former pioneer of the Glasgow Media Group, and a journalist turned academic – provides good historical context for the current debates on technology and media which highlights the need for a historical perspective that can alert us to the circularity and repetitiveness of debate based on anecdote and personal experience rather than on longer empirical accounts of news media developments under the influence of technology. Not wasting time on these recurring anxieties allows us to consider the real challenges and gives us an opportunity for an informed debate on the state of journalism today. Exploring such issues highlights the importance of studying rather than simply consuming journalism and therefore the importance and contemporary relevance of Journalism Studies.

FURTHER READING

There is a plethora of excellent reflective material published, much of which is referred to in the preceding chapter. In addition, interested readers can get a better understanding of how these discussions are developing by starting with:

Allan and Thorsen (2009) *Citizen Journalism: Global perspectives*, Peter Lang, looks at the rise of engaged citizen journalism enabled by new technologies of communication across borders.

Craig (2010) *Excellence in Online Journalism: Exploring current practices in an evolving environment*, Sage, is based upon in-depth interviews with over thirty journalists in matching the practicalities of the present with assessments of the critical discussion of the implications of these practices for journalism as a whole.

Cushion and Lewis (2010) *The Rise of 24-Hour News: Global perspectives*, Peter Lang, is a wide-ranging and empirically driven account of the limitations of this form of television news and has a full critique of how 'rolling news' can be seen as undermining the prospect of a better-informed television audience.

Jones and Salter (2011) *Digital Journalism*, Sage makes the point that in this new technological environment we are not simply talking about journalism having migrated to a new technological environment but that journalism has in fact become 'digital'.

Kaye and Quinn (2010) *Funding Journalism in the Digital Age: Business models, strategies, issues and trends*, Peter Lang, explores the conflict between quality and expense in the new economic environment partly determined by technological developments and how they have been seized upon as money-saving rather than quality-enhancing tools in the age of austerity. The authors draw on examples from as diverse a set of nations as the UK, the USA, Singapore, Norway and South Korea.

Meikle and Redden (2010) *News Online: Transformations and continuities*, Palgrave Macmillan, presents an interesting account which demonstrates how change in the contemporary world of journalism is still rooted as ever before in the contours of existing practice.

Meltzer (2010) *TV News Anchors and Journalistic Tradition: How journalists adapt to technology*, Peter Lang, explores how the internet and mobile technologies are affecting the role and function of the television news anchor, possibly the most visible and contentious aspect of television journalism. It places these contemporary challenges firmly within a tradition of critical reflection upon the status of anchors within the journalism community and the threats posed to the authority and identity of journalism in the modern age.

Pavlik (2001) *Journalism and New Media*, Columbia University Press, was the first really extensive assessment of the impact of online technologies on journalism.

Rosenberry and St John II (eds) (2010) *Public Journalism 2.0: The promise and reality of a citizen-engaged press*, Routledge, assess the enthusiasms sometimes attached to public participation in the newsgathering and reporting processes.

Rudin (2011) *Broadcasting in the 21st Century*, Palgrave Macmillan, provides an excellent survey of the opportunities for broadcasting, including journalism in the multimedia environment of the twenty-first century.

Siapera (2011) *Understanding New Media*, Sage. Provides an account of new media broad enough to encompass the way that journalism is losing its distinctiveness in the cross-currents between various new media forms and channels, especially those categorized as 'social media'.

Singer, Domingo, Hermida, Heinone, Pulussen and Quandt (2001) *Participatory Journalism: Guarding Open Gates at Online Newspapers*, John Wiley and Sons. This is a fine tour of many of the most vital questions for both journalism and its economic models. It poses questions such as who makes the news in a digital age and what legitimacy they can claim. It charts the changing relationship between online media and their audience and how social media are impacting upon the content of journalism and the behaviour and even definitions of the journalists. It calls for a shift in conceptual approaches to most traditional aspects of journalism.

BIBLIOGRAPHY

Adburgham, A. (1972) *Women in Print: Writing women and women's magazines from the Restoration to the accession of Victoria*. London: Allen and Unwin

Adie, K. (2002) *The Kindness of Strangers*. London: Hodder

Ainley, B. (1998) *Black Journalists, White Media*. Stoke-on-Trent: Trentham Books

Alagiah, G. (1999) 'New Light on Dark Continent', *Guardian* Media Section, 3 May, pp. 4–5

Aldridge, M. (2007) *Understanding the Local Media*. Maidenhead: Open University Press

Allan, R. (2005) 'Preparing Reflective Practitioners', in R. Keeble (ed.) *Print Journalism: A critical introduction*. Abingdon: Routledge, pp. 317–28

Allan, S. (1999) *News Culture*. Milton Keynes: Open University Press

Allan, S. (2005) *Journalism: Critical issues*. Maidenhead: Open University Press

Allan, S. (ed.) (2009) *The Routledge Companion to News and Journalism*. Abingdon: Routledge

Allan, S. and Thorsen, E. (2009) *Citizen Journalism: Global perspectives*. Oxford: Peter Lang

Allan, S. and Zelizer, B. (eds) (2004) *Reporting War: Journalism in wartime*. London: Routledge

Altheide, D.A. (2010) *Terror Post 9/11 and the Media*. Oxford: Peter Lang

Anderson, P.J. and Ward, G. (2006) *The Future of Journalism in the Advanced Democracies*. Aldershot: Ashgate

Anderson, P. and Weymouth, A. (1999) *Insulting the Public? The British press and the European Union*. London: Longman

Andrews, A. (2000 [1847]) *The History of British Journalism: From the foundation of the newspaper press in England to the repeal of the Stamp Act in 1855, with sketches of press celebrities*, 2 vols. London: Routledge/Thoemmes

Angell, N. (1923) *The Press and the Organisation of Society*. London: Labour Publishing Company

Atton, C. and Downing, J.F. (2008) *Alternative Journalism*. London: Sage

Atton, C. and Hamilton, J. (2008) *Alternative Journalism*. London: Sage

Atwood, R.A. and DeBeer, R.S. (2001) 'The Roots of Academic Research: Tobias Peucer's *De Relationibus Novellis* (1690)'. *Journalism Studies*. 2 (4): 485-496

Atwood, R.A. (2001) 'Tobias Peucer: De relationibus novellis'. *Journalism Studies*, 2 (4): 485–96

Bailey, M. (2009) *Narrating Media History*. Abingdon: Routledge

Baistow, T. (1985) *Fourth Rate Estate*. London: Comedia

Barber, B. (1995) *Jihad vs MacWorld: How globalism and tribalism are reshaping the world*. New York: Ballantine

Barlow, D.M., Mitchell, P. and O'Malley, T. (2005) *The Media in Wales: Voices of a small nation*. Cardiff: University of Wales Press

Barnett, S. (2006) 'Reasons to be cheerful'. *British Journalism Review*, 17 (1): 7–14

Barnett, S. and Gaber, I. (2001) *Westminster Tales: The twenty-first century crisis in British journalism*. London: Continuum

Barnett, S. and Seymour, E. (1999) *A Shrinking Iceberg Travelling South*. London: Campaign for Quality Television

Barnhurst, K. and Nerone, J. (2002) *The Form of News: A history*. New York: Guilford Press

Barry, A. (1988) 'Black Mythologies: Representation of black people on British television', in Twitchin, J. (ed.) *The Black and White Media Book*. Stoke-on-Trent: Trentham Books, pp. 83–102

Barthes, R. (1974) *Mythologies*. New York: Wang

Beaman, J. (2000) *Interviewing for Radio*. London: Routledge

Beckett, C. (2008) *SuperMedia: Saving journalism so it can save the world*. Oxford: Wiley-Blackwell

Beetham, M. (1996) *A Magazine of her Own? Domesticity and desire in the women's magazine 1800–1914*. London: Routledge

Behr, E. (1982) *Anyone Here Been Raped and Speaks English?* London: New English Library

Bell, M. (1995) *In Harm's Way: Reflections of a war zone thug*. London: Hamish Hamilton

Bell, M. (1998) 'The Journalism of Attachment', in Kiernan, M. (ed.) *Media Ethics*. London: Routledge, pp. 16–22

Belsey, A. and Chadwick, R. (1992) *Ethical Issues in Journalism and the Media*. London: Routledge

Benwell, B. (2003) *Masculinity and Men's Lifestyle Magazines*. Oxford: Blackwell

Berger, G. (2009) 'How the Internet Impacts on International News: Exploring paradoxes of the most global medium in a time of "hyperlocalism"'. *International Communication Gazette*, 71 (5): 355–71

Berger, P.L. and Luckman, T. (1967) *The Social Construction of Reality*. Harmondsworth: Penguin

Berglez, P. (2008) 'What is Global Journalism?' *Journalism Studies* 9 (6): 845–58

Berkowitz, D.A. (2010) *Cultural Meanings of News*. London: Sage

Bingham, A. (2004) *Gender, Modernity and the Popular Press in Inter-War Britain*. Oxford: Oxford University Press

Bingham, A. (2007) 'Drinking in the Last Chance Saloon: The British press and the crisis of self-regulation, 1989–95'. *Media History* 13 (1): 79–82

Bingham, A. (2009) *Family Newspapers? Sex, private life and the British popular press 1918–1978*. Oxford: Oxford University Press

Bingham, A. and Conboy, M. (2009). 'The *Daily Mirror* and the Creation of a Commercial Popular Language: A people's war and a people's paper?' *Journalism Studies*, 10 (5): 639–54

Biressi, A. and Nunn, H. (2007) (eds) *The Tabloid Culture Reader*. Milton Keynes: Open University Press

Blain, N. and Hutchinson, D. (eds) (2008) *The Media in Scotland*. Edinburgh: Edinburgh University Press

Blumler, J.G. and Franklin, B. (1990) 'Monitoring the Public Experiment in Televising the Commons: The final report', in *First Report of the Select Committee on Televising of Proceedings*. Cmnd 265-1. London: HMSO, pp. 8–68

Blumler, J.G. and Gurevitch, M. (1981) 'Politicians and the Press: An essay in role relationships', in D. Nimmo and K.R. Sanders (eds) *Handbook of Political Communication*. London: Sage

Blumler, J.G. and Gurevitch, M. (1995) *The Crisis of Political Communication*. London: Routledge

Blumler, J.G. and McQuail, D. (1968) *Television in Politics*. London: Faber and Faber

Bourdieu, P. (1998) *On Television and Journalism*. London: Pluto

Bourne, H.R.F. (2000 [1887]) *English Newspapers*, 2 vols. London: Routledge/Thoemmes

Boyce, G. (1978) 'The Fourth Estate: The reappraisal of a concept', in G. Boyce, J. Curran and P. Wingate (eds) *Newspaper History: From the seventeenth century to the present day*. London: Constable, pp. 19–40

Boyce, G., Curran, J. and Wingate, P. (eds) (1978) *Newspaper History: From the seventeenth century to the present day*. London: Constable

Boyd, A. (1988) *Broadcast Journalism: Techniques of television and radio news*. Oxford: Butterworth Heinemann

Boyd-Barrett, O. (1977a) *Mass communications in cross-cultural contexts: The case of the Third World*. Milton Keynes: Open University Press.

Boyd-Barrett, O. (1977b) 'The Collection of Foreign News in the National Press: Organisation and resources' (Working Paper 3), in O. Boyd Barrett, C. Seymour-Ure, and J. Tunstall, (eds) *Studies on the Press*. London: HMSO, pp. 15–43

Boyd-Barrett, O. (1977c) 'Media Imperialism: Towards an international framework for the analysis of media system', in J. Curran, M. Gurevitch and J. Woollacott (eds) *Mass Communication and Society*. London: Edward Arnold/The Open University Press, pp. 116–35

Boyd-Barrett, O. (1978) 'Market Control and Wholesale News: The case of Reuters', in Boyce, G., Curran, J and Wingate, P (eds) *Newspaper History: From the Seventeenth century to the present day*. London: Constable, pp. 192–204

Boyd-Barrett, O. (1980) *The International News Agencies*. London: Constable

Boyd-Barrett, O. (1997) 'Global News Wholesalers as Agents of Globalisation', in A. Sreberny-Mohammadi, D. Winseck, J. Mckenna and O. Boyd-Barrett (eds) *Media in Global Context: A reader*. London: Hodder Arnold, pp. 131–44

Boyd-Barrett, O. (1998) 'Global News Agencies', in O. Boyd-Barrett and T. Rantanen (eds) *The Globalization of News*. London: Sage, pp. 19–34

Boyd-Barrett, O. and Rantanen, T. (1998) *The Globalization of News*. London: Sage

Brake, L. (1988) 'The Old Journalism and the New: forms of cultural production in London in the 1880s', in J.H. Wiener (ed.) *Papers for the Millions: The new journalism in Britain, 1850 to 1914*. New York: Greenwood Press, pp. 1–24

Brake, L. and Demoor, M. (eds) (2009) *The Dictionary of Nineteenth Century Journalism in Great Britain and Ireland*. Gent and London: Academia Press and the British Library

Briggs, A. (1961) *The History of Broadcasting in the United Kingdom, Vol. 1: The Birth of Broadcasting*. Oxford: Oxford University Press

Briggs, A. (1965) *The History of Broadcasting in the United Kingdom, Vol. 2: The Golden Age of the Wireless*. Oxford: Oxford University Press

Briggs, A. (1970a) *The History of Broadcasting in the United Kingdom, Vol. 3: The War of Words*. Oxford: Oxford University Press

Briggs, A. (1970b) *The History of Broadcasting in the United Kingdom, Vol.4: Sound and Vision*. Oxford: Oxford University Press

Briggs, A. (1995) *The History of Broadcasting in the United Kingdom, Vol. 5: Competition*. Oxford: Oxford University Press

Brighton, P. and Foy, D. (2007) *News Values*. London: Sage

Bromley, M. (1997) 'The End of Journalism? Changes in workplace practices in the press and broadcasting in the 1990s', in M. Bromley and T. O'Malley (eds) *A Journalism Reader*. London: Routledge. pp. 330–50

Bromley, M. (ed.) (2001) *No News Is Bad News*. Harlow: Pearson Education

Bromley, M. and Tumber, H. (1997) 'From Fleet Street to Cyberspace: The British "popular" press in the late twentieth century'. *European Journal of Communication Studies*, 22 (3): 365–78

Brookes, H. (1995) 'Suit, Tie and a Touch of Ju-Ju – The Ideological Construction of Africa: A critical discourse analysis of news on Africa in the British press'. *Discourse and Society* 6 (4): 461–94

Brown, L. (1985) *Victorian News and Newspapers*. Oxford: Clarendon Press

Burns, G. (2008) *Born Yesterday: The news as a novel*. London: Faber and Faber

Burns, T. (1977) *The BBC: Public institution and private world*. London: Macmillan

Cameron, D. (1996) 'Style Policy and Style Politics: A neglected aspect of the language of the news'. *Media, Culture and Society* 18: 315–33

Cameron, J. (1997) 'Journalism: A trade', in J. Cameron, *Point of Departure*. London: Arthur Baker. Reprinted in M. Bromley and T. O'Malley (1997) (eds) *A Journalism Reader*. London: Routledge, pp. 170–3

Candlin, E.F. (1951) *Teach Yourself Journalism*. London: English University Books

Carey, J. (1989) *Communication as Culture: Essays on media and society*. Boston, MA: Hyman

Carruthers, S. (2000) *The Media at War*. London: Palgrave

Carter, C., Allen, S. and Branston, G. (eds) (1998) *News, Gender and Power*. London: Routledge

Castells, M. (1996) *The Rise of the Network Society*. Oxford: Blackwell

Chalaby, J. (1998) *The Invention of Journalism*. Basingstoke: Macmillan

Chalaby, J. (2000) 'Northcliffe: Proprietor as journalist', in P. Caterall, C. Seymour-Ure and A. Smith (eds) *Northcliffe's Legacy: Aspects of the British popular press 1896–1996*. Basingstoke: Macmillan, pp. 27–44

Chalkley, A. (1970) *A Manual of Development Journalism*. New Delhi: Vikas

Chambers, D., Steiner, L. and Fleming, C. (2004) *Women and Journalism*. London: Routledge

Chapman, J. (2005) *Comparative Media History: An introduction – 1789 to the present*. London: Polity

Chibnall, S. (1977) *Law and Order News*. London: Tavistock

Chilton, P. (1982) 'Nukespeak: Nuclear language, culture and propaganda', in C. Aubrey (ed.) *Nukespeak: The media and the bomb*. London: Comedia, pp. 94–112

Chippendale, P. and Horrie, C. (1992) *Stick It Up Your Punter! The rise and fall of the Sun*. London: Mandarin

Christmas, L. (1997) *Chaps of Both Sexes? Women decision-makers in newspapers: do they make a difference?* London: BT Forum/Women in Journalism

Cockerell, M., Hennessy, P. and Walker, D. (1984) *Sources Close to the Prime Minister*. London: Macmillan

Cohen, S. (1973) *Folk Devils and Moral Panics*. London: Paladin

Cohen, S. and Young, J. (eds) (1973) *The Manufacture of News: Social problems, deviance and the news media*. London: Constable

Cole, P. and Harcup, T. (2010) *Newspaper Journalism*. London: Sage

Conboy, M. (2002) *The Press and Popular Culture*. London: Sage

Conboy, M. (2006) *Tabloid Britain: Constructing a community through language*. Abingdon: Routledge

Conboy, M. (2011) *Journalism in Britain: A historical introduction*, London: Sage

Connell, I. (1992) 'Personalities in the Popular Media', in P. Dahlgren and C. Sparks (eds) *Journalism and Popular Culture*. London: Sage, pp. 64–83

Cottle, S. (ed.) (2003) *Media, Organization and Production*. London: Sage

Cottle, S. (2006) *Mediatized Conflict: Developments in media and conflict studies*. Maidenhead: Open University Press

Cottle, S. (2009) 'Journalism Studies: Coming of (global) age'. *Journalism: Theory, Practice and Criticism* (Special 10th anniversary issue) 10 (3): 309–11

Craig, D.A. (2010) *Excellence in Online Journalism: Exploring current practices in an evolving environment*. London: Sage

Cranfield, G.A. (1962) *The Development of the Provincial Newspaper 1700–1760*. Oxford. Clarendon

Cranfield, G.A. (1976) *The Press and Society*. London: Longman

Crisell, A. (1994) *Understanding Radio*. London: Routledge

Crisell, A. (1997) *An Introductory History of British Broadcasting*. London: Routledge

Crisell, A. and Starkey, G. (2009) *Radio Journalism*. London: Sage

Critcher, C. (2003) *Moral Panics and the Media*. Buckingham: Open University Press

Critcher, C., Parker, M. and Sondhi, R. (1975) *Race in the Provincial Press*. Birmingham: University of Birmingham, Centre for Contemporary Cultural Studies

Cudlipp, H. (1953) *Publish and Be Damned*. London: Andrew Dakers

Curran, J. (2002) 'Media and the making of British society *c.* 1700–2000'. *Media History*, 8 (2): 135–54

Curran, J. (2009) 'Narratives of Media History Revisited', in M. Bailey (ed.) *Narrating Media History*. Abingdon: Routledge, pp. 1–21

Curran, J. and Park, M.-J. (eds) (2000) *De-Westernizing Media Studies*. London: Routledge

Curran, J. and Seaton, J. (1981) *Power without Responsibility: The press and broadcasting in Britain*. London: Fontana

Curran, J., Douglas, A. and Whannel, G. (1980) 'The Political Economy of the Human-Interest Story', in A. Smith (ed.) *Newspapers and Democracy*. Cambridge, MA: MIT Press, pp. 288–342

Cushion, S. and Lewis, J. (2010) *The Rise of 24-Hour Television News: Global perspectives*. New York: Peter Lang

Cushion, S., Lewis, J. and Ramsay, G. (2010) *Four Nations Impartiality Review Follow-up: An analysis of reporting devolution*. London: BBC Trust Publications

Dahlgren, P. (1992) 'Introduction', in P. Dahlgren and C. Sparks (eds) *Journalism and Popular Culture*. London: Sage, pp. 1–23

Dahlgren, P. and Sparks, C. (eds) (1992) *Journalism and Popular Culture*. London: Sage

Davies, N. (2008) *Flat Earth News*. London: Chatto and Windus

Davis, A. (2002) *Public Relations Democracy: Public relations, politics and the mass media in Britain*. Manchester: Manchester University Press

Deacon, D., Pickering, M., Golding, P. and Murdock, G. (1999) *Researching Communications*. London: Arnold

de Bruin, M. (2000) 'Gender, Organisational and Professional Identities in Journalism'. *Journalism: Theory, Practice and Criticism* 1 (2): 217–38

de Burgh, H. (2000) *Investigative Journalism: Context and practice*. London: Routledge

de Burgh, H. (ed.) (2005) *Making Journalists*. Abingdon: Routledge

Delano, A. (2003) 'Women journalists: What's the difference?' *Journalism Studies*, 4 (2): 273–86

Delano, A. (2008) 'Different horses, different courses'. *British Journalism Review*, 19 (4): 68–74

Delano, A. and Henningham, J. (1995) *The News Breed: British journalists in the 1990s*. London: London Institute

Deuze, M. (2002) 'National News Cultures: Towards a profile of journalists using cross-national survey findings'. *Journalism and Mass Communication Quarterly*, 79 (1): 134–49

van Dijk, T. (1993) *Elite Discourse and Racism*: London: Sage

Doyle, G. (2003) *Media Ownership*. London: Sage

Edelmann, M. (1966) *The Mirror: A political history*. London: Hamish Hamilton

Elliott, P. (1974) 'Mass Communication and Social Change: The imagery of development and the development of imagery', in E. de Kadt and G. Williams (eds) *The Sociology of Development*. London: Tavistock, pp. 229–54

Elliott, P. (1980) 'Press Performance as Political Ritual', in H. Christian (ed.) *The Sociology of Journalism and the Press* (Sociological Review Monograph 29). Keele: University of Keele, pp. 141–77

Elliott, P. and Golding, P. (1973) 'The news media and foreign affairs', in R. Boardman and A.J.R. Groom (eds) *The Management of Britain's External Relations*. New York: Macmillan

Elliott, P. and Golding, P. (1979) *Making the News*. London: Longman

Engel, M. (1996) *Tickle the Public: One hundred years of the popular press*. London: Gollancz and Prentice Hall

Ensor, R. (1968) *The Oxford History of England*, vol. 4, 1870–1914. Oxford: Oxford University Press

Ericson, R., Baranek, P. and Chan, J. (1987) *Visualizing Deviance*. Milton Keynes: Open University Press

Esser, F. (1998) 'Editorial Structures and Work Principles in British and German Newsrooms'. *European Journal of Communication*, 13 (3): 375–405

Esser, F. (1999) ' "Tabloidization" of News: A comparative analysis of Anglo-American and German press journalism'. *European Journal of Communication*, 14 (3): 291–324

Fairclough, N. (1995) *Critical Discourse Analysis*. London: Routledge

Fairclough, N. (2000) *New Labour, New Language?* London: Routledge

Featherstone, M. (1993) *Global Culture: Nationalism, globalization and modernity*. London: Sage

Fenton, N. (ed.) (2010) *New Media, Old News: Journalism and democracy in the digital age*. London: Sage

Fish, S.E. (1976) 'Interpreting the Variorum'. *Critical Inquiry*, 2 (Spring): 465–85

Fiske, J. (1987) *Television Culture*. London: Methuen

Fiske, J. (1989) *Understanding Popular Culture*. London: Routledge

Fiske, J. (1994) *Reading the Popular*. London: Routledge

Fiske, J. and Hartley, J. (1978) *Reading Television*. London: Methuen

Fowler, R. (1991) *Language in the News: Discourse and ideology in the press*. London: Routledge

Francis, J. (2003) 'White Culture, Black Mark'. *British Journalism Review* 14 (3): 67–73

Frank, J. (1961) *The Beginnings of the English Newspaper 1620–1660*. Cambridge, MA: Harvard University Press

Franklin, B. (1994) *Packaging Politics*. London: Edward Arnold

Franklin, B. (1997) *Newszack and News Media*. London: Arnold

Franklin, B. (ed.) (2001) *British Television Policy: A reader*. London: Routledge

Franklin, B. (2004) *Packaging Politics: Political communications in Britain's media democracy*, 2nd edn. London: Arnold

Franklin, B. (ed.) (2005) *Television Policy: The MacTaggart lectures*. Edinburgh: Edinburgh University Press

Franklin, B. (ed) (2009) *Key Concepts in Public Relations*. London: Sage

Franklin, B. and Carlson, M. (2011) *Journalists, Sources and Credibility: New perspectives*. Abingdon: Routledge

Franklin, B. and Murphy, D. (1991) *What News? The market, politics and the local press*. London: Routledge

Franklin, B. and Parton, N. (eds) (1991) *Social Work, the Media and Public Relations*. London: Routledge

Franklin, B., Horgan, M., Langley, Q., Mosdell, N. and Pill, E. (2005) *Key Concepts in Public Relations*. London: Sage

Franks, S. (2005) 'Lacking a Clear Narrative: Foreign reporting after the Cold War'. *Political Quarterly*, 76 (51): 91–101

Franks, S. (2006) 'The CARMA Report: Western media coverage of humanitarian disasters', *Political Quarterly*, 77 (2): 281–4

Friedrichs, H. (1911) *The Life of Sir George Newnes*. London: Stodder and Houghton

Frölich, R. and Holtz-Bacha, C. (eds) (2003) *Journalism Education in Europe and North America: A structural comparison*. Cresskill, NJ: Hampton Press

Frost, C. (2000) *Media Ethics and Self-Regulation*. Harlow: Longman

Frost, C. (2004) 'The Press Complaints Commission: A study of ten years of adjudications on press complaints.' *Journalism Studies*, 5 (1): 101–14

Fuller, L. (2008) *Sportscasters/Sportscasting*. Abingdon: Routledge

Galtung, J. (2002) 'Peace Journalism: A challenge', in W. Kempf and H. Luostarinen (eds) *Journalism and the New Order,* vol. 2, *Studying War and Media*. Goteborg: Nordicom

Galtung, J. and Ruge, M. (1965) 'The Structure of Foreign News: The presentation of the Congo, Cuba and Cyprus crises in four Norwegian newspapers'. *Journal of International Peace Research*, 1: 64–91

Garnham, N. (1979) 'Contribution to a Political Economy of Mass Communication'. *Media, Culture and Society*, 1 (2): 123–46

Garnham, N. (1990) *Capitalism and Communication: Global culture and the economics of information*. London: Sage

Gerbner, G. and Marvanyi, G. (1983) 'The Many Worlds of International News?', in J. Richstad and M. Anderson (eds) *Crisis in International News: Policies and prospects*. New York: Columbia University Press, pp. 184–96

Glasgow Media Group (1976) *Bad News*. London: Routledge and Kegan Paul

Glasgow Media Group (2000) *Viewing the World: News content and audience studies*. London: DFID

Glasser, T. (2006) 'Journalism Studies and the Education of Journalists'. *Journalism Studies*, 7 (1): 146–9

Golding, P. (1977) 'Media Professionalism in the Third World: The transfer of an ideology', in J. Curran, M. Gurevitch and J. Woollacott (eds) *Mass Communication and Society*. London: Sage Publications, pp. 291–308

Golding, P. and Elliott, P. (1979) *Making the News*. London: Longman

Golding, P. and Harris, P. (1997) *Beyond Cultural Imperialism: Globalisation, communication and the new international order*. London: Sage

Golding, P. and Middleton (1982) *Images of Welfare: Press and public attitudes to poverty*. Oxford: Blackwell

Golding, P. and Murdock, G. (1991) 'Culture, Communications and Political Economy', in J. Curran and M. Gurevitch (eds) *Mass Media and Society*. London: Edward Arnold, pp. 70–92

Gopsill, T. and Neale, G. (2008) *Journalists: 100 Years of the NUJ*. London: Profile

Gough-Yates, A. (2003) *Understanding Women's Magazines: Publishing, markets and readerships*. London: Routledge

Gratton, C. and Solberg, H.A. (2007) *The Economics of Sports Broadcasting*. Abingdon: Routledge

Greatbatch, D. (1988) 'A Turn-Taking System for British News Interviews', in A. Bell and P. Garrett (eds) *Approaches to Media Discourse*. Oxford: Blackwell, pp. 167–85

Greater London Authority (2007) 'The Search for Common Ground: Muslims, non-Muslims and the UK media.' A report commissioned for the Mayor of London. Available at http://www.london.gov.uk/mayor/equalities/doc/commonground-report.pdf (accessed 14 July 2009)

Greenslade, R. (1996) 'The Telling Selling Game'. *Guardian* 2, 12 August, p. 17

Greenslade, R.(2004) *Press Gang: How newspapers make profits from propaganda*. London: Macmillan

Greenslade, R. (2004) 'Myth Information' *British Journalism Review*, vol. 15(3), pp. 74–76.

Greenslade, R. (2010) 'Trinity Mirror Debate: Williams defends his research in an open letter'. *Guardian*. Media supplement, 22 July. Available at http://www.guardian.co.uk/media/greenslade/2010/jul/22/local-newspapers-cardiff university (accessed 12 February 2012)

Grieve, M. (1964) *Millions Made My Story*. London: Gollancz

Gripsrud, J. (1992) 'The Aesthetics and Politics of Melodrama', in P. Dahlgren and C. Sparks (eds) *Journalism and Popular Culture*. London: Sage, pp. 84–95

Gripsrud, J. (2000) 'Tabloidization, Popular Journalism and Democracy', in C. Sparks and J. Tulloch (eds), *Tabloid Tales: Global debates over media standards*. Oxford: Rowman and Littlefield, pp. 285–300

Gumperz, J. and Hymes, D. (1972) (eds) *Directions in Sociolinguistics: The ethnography of communication*. New York: Holt, Rinehart and Winston

Gurevitch, M., Levy, M.R. and Roeh, I. (1993) 'The Global Newsroom: Convergences and diversities in the globalization of television news', in P. Dahlgren and C. Sparks (eds) *Communication and Citizenship: Journalism and the public sphere*. London: Routledge, pp. 195–216

Habermas, J. (1989) *The Structural Transformation of the Public Sphere: An inquiry into a category of bourgeois society*. Cambridge: Polity

Hackett, R. and Zhao, Y. (2005) (eds) *Democratizing Global Media: One world, many struggles*. New York: Rowman and Littlefield

Hall, S. (1973) 'Encoding/Decoding in the Television Discourse'. *CCCS Position Paper*. Birmingham: Centre for Contemporary Cultural Studies, University of Birmingham

Hall, S. and Jacques, M. (1983) 'Introduction', in M. Jacques (ed.) *New Times: The changing face of politics in the 1990s*. London: Wishart and Lawrence, pp. 11–20

Hall, S., Critcher, C., Jefferson, T., Clarke, J. and Roberts, B. (1978) *Policing the Crisis: Mugging, the state and law and order*. Basingstoke: Macmillan

Hallin, D.C. (1994) *We Keep America on Top of the World*. Oxford: Oxford University Press

Hallin, D.C. and Mancini, P. (2004) *Comparing Media Systems: Three models of media and politics*. Cambridge: Cambridge University Press

Halloran, J., Elliot, P. and Murdock, G. (1970) *Demonstrations and Communication*. Harmondsworth: Penguin

Hamilton, J.T. and Lawrence, R. (2010) 'Bridging Past and Future: Using history and practice to inform social scientific study of foreign newsgathering'. *Journalism Studies*, 11(5): 683–99

Hampton, M. (2004) *Visions of the Press in Britain 1850–1950*. Champaign, IL: University of Illinois Press

Hanitzsch, T. (2011) 'Mapping Journalism Cultures Across Nations: A comparative study of 18 countries'. *Journalism Studies*, 12 (3): 273–92

Hanna, M. (2008) 'Universities as Evangelists of the Watchdog Role', in: H. de Burgh (ed.) *Investigative Journalism: Context and practice*, 2nd edn. Abingdon: Routledge, pp. 157–73

Hanna, M. and Banks, D. (2009) *McNae's Essential Law for Journalists*, 20th edn. Oxford: Oxford University Press

Hanna, M. and Sanders, K. (2007) 'Journalism Education in Britain'. *Journalism Practice*, 1 (3): 404–20

Hansen, A., Cottle, S., Negrine, R. and Newbold, C. (1998) *Mass Communications Research*. Basingstoke: Palgrave Macmillan

Harcup, T. (2001) *Journalism: Principles and practice*. London: Sage

Harcup, T. and O'Neill, D. (2001). 'What is News? Galtung and Ruge revisited'. *Journalism Studies*, 2 (2): 261–80

Hargreaves, I. (2002) *Journalists at Work*. London: Publishing NTO/Skillset

Hargreaves, I. (2005) *Journalism: A very short introduction*. Oxford: Oxford University Press

Hargreaves, I. and Thomas, J. (2002) *New News, Old News*. London: Independent Television Commission/British Standards Commission Research Publication

Harrington, S. (2008) 'Popular News in the 21st Century: Time for a new critical approach'. *Journalism: Theory, Practice and Criticism*, 9 (3): 266–84

Harris, P. (1981) *Reporting Southern Africa: Western news agencies reporting from southern Africa*. Paris: UNESCO

Harrison, J. (2006) *News*. Abingdon: Routledge

Harrison, J. (2010) 'UGC and Gatekeeping at the BBC', *Journalism Studies*, 11 (2): 243–56

Harrison, M. (1985) *Television News: Whose bias?* Newbury: Policy Journals

Harrison, P. and Palmer, R. (1986) *News Out of Africa*. London: Hilary Shipman

Harrison, S. (1974) *Poor Men's Guardians*. London: Lawrence and Wishart

Hartley, J. (1982) *Understanding News*. London: Methuen

Hartley, J. (1996) *Popular Reality*. London: Arnold

Headrick, D. (1981) *The Tools of Empire*. Oxford: Oxford University Press

Heller, Z. (1999) 'Girl Columns', in S. Glover (ed.) *Secrets of the Press: Journalists on journalism*. Harmondsworth: Penguin, pp. 10–17

Hemmingway, E. (2007) *Into the Newsroom: Exploring the digital production of regional television news*. Abingdon: Routledge

Hendy, D. (2007) *Life on Air: A history of Radio Four*. Oxford: Oxford University Press

Herd, H. (1952) *The March of Journalism: The story of the British press from 1622 to the present day*. London: Allen and Unwin

Heritage, J. (1985) 'Analysing News Interviews: Aspects of the production of talk for an overhearing audience', in T. van Dijk (ed.) *Handbook of Discourse Analysis: Discourse and Dialogue*. London: Academic Press, pp. 95–119

Herman, E. and Chomsky, N. (1988) *Manufacturing Consent: The political economy of the mass media*. New York: Pantheon Books

Herman, E. and McChesney, R. (1997) *The Global Media: The new missionaries of global capitalism*. Washington, DC: Cassell

Hermes, J. (1995) *Reading Women's Magazines: An analysis of everyday media use*. Cambridge: Polity Press

Hermida, A. (2010) 'Twittering the News: The emergence of ambient journalism'. *Journalism Practice*, 4 (3): 297–308

Hermida, A. and Thurmin, J. (2008) 'A Clash of Cultures: The integration of user-generated content within professional journalistic frameworks at British newspapers'. *Journalism Practice*, 2 (3): 343–56

Hill, A. (2005) *Reality Television*. Abingdon: Routledge

Hobsbawm, J. (ed.) (2006) *Where the Truth Lies: Trust and morality in PR and journalism*. London: Atlantic

Hodge, R. and Kress, G. (1979) *Language as Ideology*. London: Routledge

Hoggart, R. (1957) *The Uses of Literacy*. Harmondsworth: Pelican

Holland, P. (1983) 'The Page 3 Girl Speaks to Women Too'. *Screen*, 24 (3): 84–102

Holland, P. (1998). 'The Politics of the Smile: "Soft news" and the sexualization of the popular press', in C. Carter, G. Branston and S. Allen (eds) *News, Gender and Power*. London: Routledge, pp. 17–32

Holmes, T. (2007) 'Special Issue: Mapping the magazine'. *Journalism Studies*, 8 (4)

Holmes, T. and Nice, L. (2011) *Magazine Journalism*. London: Sage

Horrie, C. (2003) *Tabloid Nation: From the birth of the* Mirror *to the death of the tabloid*. London: André Deutsch

Hoyer, S. and Pöttker, H. (2005) *The Diffusion of the News Paradigm 1850–2000*. Gothenburg: Nordicom.

Hunt, L. (1998) *British Low Culture: From safari suits to sexploitation*. London: Routledge

Inglis, F. (2002) *People's Witness: The journalist in modern politics*. New Haven, CT: Yale University Press

Innis, H.A. (1951) *The Bias of Communication*. Toronto: University of Toronto Press

Innis, H.A. (1972) *Empire and Communication*. Toronto: University of Toronto Press

Jackson, P., Stevenson, N. and Brooks, K. (eds) (2001) *Making Sense of Men's Magazines*. Cambridge: Polity

Jempson, M. and Cookson, R. (eds) (2004) *Satisfaction Guaranteed? Press complaints systems under scrutiny*. Bristol: Mediawise

Johnston, J.W.C., Slawski, E.J. and Bowman, W.W. (1976) *The News People: A sociological portrait of American journalists and their work*. Urbana, IL: University of Illinois Press

Jones, A. (1996) *Powers of the Press: Newspapers, power and the public in nineteenth century England*. Aldershot: Scolar Press

Jones, L. and Salter, J. (2011) *Digital Journalism*. London: Sage

Jones, N. (1995) *Soundbites and Spin Doctors: How politicians manipulate the media and vice versa*. London: Cassell

Jonson, B. ([1631]2002) *The Staple of News*, ed. A. Parr Manchester: Manchester University Press,

Josephi, B. (ed.) (2010) *Journalism Education in Countries with Limited Media Freedom*. New York: Peter Lang

Kadritzke, S. (2000) 'Reporting the News: Does the targeting of an audience affect the informational value of television news?' MA Thesis, Trinity and All Saints University College, Leeds.

Kariithi, N. (1994) 'The Crisis Facing Developing Journalism in Africa'. *Media Development*, 4: 28–30

Kaul, C. (2003) *Reporting the Raj: The British press and India c.1880–1922*. Manchester: Manchester University Press

Kaye, J. and Quinn, S. (2010) *Funding Journalism in the Digital Age: Business models, strategies, issues and trends*. Oxford: Peter Lang

Keeble, R. (1994) *The Newspapers Handbook*. London: Routledge

Keeble, R. (1997) *Secret State: Silent Press*. Luton: University of Luton Press

Keeble, R. (2001) *Ethics for Journalists*. London: Routledge

Keeble, R.(2005a) 'New Militarism, Massacrespeak and the language of silence'. *Ethical Space: The International Journal of Communication Ethics*, 2 (1): 39–45

Keeble, R. (2005b) *Print Journalism: A critical introduction*. Abingdon: Routledge

Keeble, R., Tulloch, J. and Zollman, F. (2010) *Peace Journalism: War and conflict resolution*. Oxford: Peter Lang

Kellner, P. (1983) 'The lobby, official secrets and good government'. *Parliamentary Affairs*, 36 (1): 275–81

Kiernan, V. (1969) *The Lords of Human Kind: European attitudes to other cultures in the imperial age*, 2nd edn. London: Weidenfeld and Nicolson

King, E. and Chapman, J. (2011) *Key Readings in Journalism*. Abingdon: Routledge

Knightley, P. (1975) *The First Casualty: The war reporter as hero, propaganda and myth maker*. London: André Deutsch

Knightley, P. (2004) *The First Casualty: The war reporter as hero, propaganda and myth maker, from the Crimea to Iraq*. Baltimore, MD: Johns Hopkins University Press

Koss, S. (1981) *The Rise and Fall of the Political Press in Britain*, vol. 1, *The Nineteenth Century*. London: Hamilton

Koss, S. (1984) *The Rise and Fall of the Political Press in Britain*, vol. 2, *The Twentieth Century*. London: Hamilton

L'Etaing, J. (2004) *Public Relations in Britain: A history of professional practice in the twentieth century*. London: Routledge

Labov, W. (1972) *Language in the Inner City*. Philadelphia, PA: University of Pennsylvania Press

Lamb, L. (1989) *Sunrise: The remarkable rise and rise of the best-selling, soaraway* Sun. London: Papermac

Langer, J. (1998) *Tabloid Television: Popular journalism and the 'other' news*. London: Routledge

Lee-Wright, P., Phillips, A. and Witschge, T. (2012) *Changing Journalism*. Abingdon: Routledge

Leslie, A. (2004) 'If the BBC is wrecked or ever weakened by bullying politicians, then we WILL all be losers'. *Daily Mail*, 30 January. p. 12

Levy, D.A.L. and Nielsen, R.K. (2010) (eds) *The Changing Business of Journalism and Its Implications for Democracy*. Oxford: Oxford University Press

Littleton, (1992) *The Wapping Dispute: An examination of the conflict and its impact on the national newspaper industry*. Aldershot: Avebury

Lloyd, J. (2004) *What the Media Are Doing to Our Politics*. London: Constable and Robinson

Löffelholz, M. and Weaver, D. (eds) (2008) *Global Journalism Research*. Oxford: Blackwell

Lynch, J. and McGoldrick, A. (2005) *Peace Journalism*. Stroud: Hawthorn Press

MacArthur, B. (1988) *Eddy Shah,* Today *and the Newspaper Revolution*. London: David and Charles

MacGregor, S. (2002) *Woman of Today*. London: Headline

McKay, J. (2000) *The Magazines Handbook*. London: Routledge

McKee, A. (2005) *The Public Sphere: An introduction*. Melbourne: Cambridge University Press

MacKenzie, J. (1984) *Propaganda and Empire*. Manchester: Manchester University Press

MacKenzie, J. (1986) *Imperialism and Popular Culture*. Manchester: Manchester University Press

McKnight, D. (2003) '"A world hungry for a new philosophy": Rupert Murdoch and the rise of neo-liberalism'. *Journalism Studies*, 4 (3): 347–58

McLachlan, S. and Golding. P. (2000) 'Tabloidization in the British Press: A quantitative investigation into changes in British newspapers', in C. Sparks and J. Tulloch (eds) *Tabloid Tales: Global debates over media standards*. Oxford: Rowman and Littlefield, pp. 75–90

McLoughlin, L. (2000) *The Language of Magazines*. London: Routledge

McLuhan, M. (1964) *Understanding the Media: The extensions of man*. New York: McGraw Hill

McNair, B. (1994) *News and Journalism in the UK*. London: Routledge (5th edn 2009)

McNair, B. (1998) *The Sociology of Journalism*. London: Routledge

McNair, B. (2000) *Journalism and Democracy: An evaluation of the political public sphere*. London: Routledge

McNair, B. (2003) 'From Control to Chaos: Towards a new sociology of journalism'. *Media, Culture and Society*, 25 (4): 547–555

McNair, B. (2003) *An Introduction to Political Communication*. London: Routledge

McNair, B. (2006) *Cultural Chaos: Journalism, news and power in a globalized world*. Abindgon: Routledge

McNair, B. (2010) *Journalists in Film: Heroes and villains*. Edinburgh: Edinburgh University Press

McQuail, D. (2008) *McQuail's Mass Communication Theory*, 5th edn. London: Sage

Macaulay, T. (1828) "Hallam's constitutional history". *The Edinburgh Review*, 8: p. 165

Machin, D. and Niblock, S. (2006) *News Production: Theory and practice*. Abingdon: Routledge

Mansfield, F. (1936) *The Complete Journalist: A study of the principles and practice of newspaper making*. London: Sir Isaac Pitman

Marr, A. (2005) *My Trade: A short history of British journalism*. London: Pan

Marsh, K. (2004) 'Power but scant responsibility'. *British Journalism Review* 15 (4): 17–21

Marshall, P. D. (2010) 'The Promotion and Presentation of the Self: Celebrity as marker of presentational media'. *Celebrity Studies*, 1 (1): 35–48

Martin, B. (2011) *Magazines: A guide to critical practice*. Abingdon: Routledge

Matheson, D. and Allan, S. (2009) *Digital War Reporting*. Cambridge: Polity

Matthews, R. (forthcoming 2013) *Provincial Newspapers: A story worth telling*. London: Continuum

Meikle, G. and Redden, G. (2010) *News Online: Transformation and continuities*. Basingstoke: Palgrave Macmillan

Meltzer, K. (2010) *TV News Anchors and Journalistic Tradition: How journalists adapt to technology*. Oxford: Peter Lang

Mercer, D., Mungham, G. and Williams, K. (1987) *The Fog of War*. London: Heinemann

Miller, D. (2004) *Tell Me Lies: Propaganda and media distortion in the attack on Iraq*. London: Pluto Press

Miller, D. and Dinan, W. (2008) *A Century of Spin: How public relations became the cutting edge of corporate power*. London: Pluto

Montgomery, M. (2007) *The Discourse of Broadcast News: A linguistic approach*. Abingdon: Routledge

Morison, S. (1932) *The English Newspaper: Some account of the physical development of journals printed in London between 1622 and the present day*. Cambridge. Cambridge University Press

Morrish, J. and Bradshaw, P. (2011) *Magazine Editing*, 3rd edn. Abingdon: Routledge

Morrison, D. and Tumber, H. (1988) *Journalists at War: The dynamics of war reporting during the Falklands War*. London: Sage

Muhlmann, G. (2008) *A Political History of Journalism*. Cambridge: Polity

Murphy, D. (1976) *The Silent Watchdog*. London: Constable

Nadoo, A. (2009) *Hearts Exposed: Transplants and the media in 1960s Britain*. Basingstoke: Palgrave Macmillan

National Council for Civil Liberties (1986) *No Way in Wapping: Effect of the policing of the news international dispute on Wapping residents*. Civil Liberties Trust

Negrine, R. (1989) *Politics and the Mass Media in Britain*. London: Routledge

Negrine, R., Holtz-Bacha, C., Mancini, P. and Papathanassopoulos, S. (eds) (2006) *The Professionalization of Political Communication in Europe*. Bristol: Intellect Publishers

Nerone, J. (1987) 'The Mythology of the Penny Press'. *Critical Studies in Media Communication*, 4 (4): 376–404

Niblock, S. (2006) *News Production: Theory and practice*. Abingdon: Routledge

Niblock, S. (2010) *Journalism: A beginner's guide*. Oxford: One World Publications

Niblock, S. and Machin, D. (2007) 'News production in a Digital Newsroom: Inside independent radio news'. *Journalism: Theory, Practice and Criticism*, 8 (2): 184–204

Niblock, S. and Machin, D. (2008) 'Branding Newspapers: Visual texts as social practice'. *Journalism Studies*, 9 (2): 244–59 de Nie, M. (2004) *The Eternal Paddy: Irish identity and the British press, 1798–1882*. Madison, WI: University of Winconsin Press

Nkrumah, K. (1965) *The African Journalist*. Dar-es-Salaam: Tanzania Publishers

Nossek, H. (2004) 'Our News and Their News: The role of national identity in the coverage of foreign news'. *Journalism Theory and Practice*, 5 (3): 343–68

Oborne, P. (1999) *Alastair Campbell: New Labour and the art of media management*. London: Aurum

O'Malley, T. (1994) *Closedown: The BBC and government broadcasting policy*. London: Pluto Press

O'Malley, T. (2001) 'The Decline of Public Service Broadcasting in the UK, 1979–2000', in M. Bromley (ed.) *No News Is Bad News*. Harlow: Pearson, pp. 28–45

O'Neill, D. and O'Connor, C. (2008) 'The Passive Journalist: How sources dominate local news'. *Journalism Practice*, 2 (3): 487–500

Örnebring, H. (2008) 'The Consumer as Producer – of What?' *Journalism Studies* (9)5: 771–85

Örnebring, H. (2009) 'The Two Professionalisms of Journalism: Journalism and the changing context of work'. Reuters Institute for the Study of Journalism. Working publication

Paletz, D.L. (1998) *The Media in American Politics: Contents and consequences*. New York: Longman

Palmer, M. (1978) 'The British Press and International News, 1851–99', in G. Boyce, J. Curran and P. Wingate (eds) *Newspaper History: From the seventeenth century to the present day*. London: Constable, pp. 205–19

Palmer, M. (2008) 'International News from Paris and London-based Newsrooms'. *Journalism Studies*, 9 (5): 813–21

Park, R. E. (1925) 'The Natural History of the Newspaper', in R.E. Park, E.W. Burgess and R.D. McKenzie (eds) *The City*. Chicago, IL: Chicago University Press

Paterson, C. and Sreberny, A. (eds) (2004) *International News in the Twenty-First Century*. Luton: John Libbey

Pavlik, J. (2001) *Journalism and New Media*. New York: Columbia University Press

Pavlik, J. (2005) 'Running the Technological Gauntlet: Journalism and new media', in H. de Burgh (ed.) *Making Journalists*. Abingdon: Routledge

Peters, B. (2001) *Equality and Quality: Setting standards for women in journalism*. IFG Survey and Report. Available at http://www.ifg.org/assets/docs/321/007/a61e5e7–2c52b07.pdf

Petley, J. (2006) 'Public Service Broadcasting in the UK', in D. Gomery and L. Hockley (eds) *Television Industry*. London: British Film Institute, pp. 42–5

Petley, J. (2008) 'Bleak Outlook on the News Front'. *British Journalism Review*, 19 (3): 19–25

Phillips, A. (2007) *Good Writing for Journalists: Narrative, style and structure*. London: Sage

Pieterse, J. (1995) *White on Black: Images of Africa and blacks in western popular culture*. New Haven, CT: Yale University Press

Pilger, J. (2001) *Heroes*. London: Vintage

Pinkus, P. (1968) *Grub Street Stripped Bare*. London: Constable

Platell, A. (1999) 'Institutionalized Sexism', in S. Glover (ed.) *Secrets of the Press: Journalists on journalism*. Harmondsworth: Penguin, pp. 140–7

Postman, N. (1986) *Amusing Ourselves to Death: Public discourse in the age of showbusiness*. London: Methuen

Potter, S. (2003) *News and The British World: The emergence of an imperial press system, 1876–1922*. Oxford: Oxford University Press

Potter, S. (ed.) (2005) *Imperial Communication: Australia, Britain and the British Empire*. London: Menzies Centre for Australian Studies

Pöttker, H. (2003) 'News and its Communicative Aspect: The inverted pyramid – when and why did it appear?' *Journalism Studies*, 4 (4): 501–11

Preston, P. (2004) 'Tabloids: Only the beginning'. *British Journalism Review*, 15 (1): 50–5

Preston, P. (2009) *Making the News: Journalism and news cultures in Europe*. Abingdon: Routledge

Quinn, F. (2011) *Law for Journalists*, 2nd edn. Harlow: Pearson Education

Randall, D. (1996) *The Universal Journalist*. London: Pluto Press

Raymond, J. (1996) *The Invention of the Newspaper: English newsbooks 1641–1649*. Oxford: Oxford University Press

Raymond, J. (ed.) (1999) *News, Newspapers and Sociey in Early Modern England*. London: Frank Cass

Read, D. (1992) *The Power of News: The history of Reuters*. Oxford: Oxford University Press

Richardson, J.E. (2004) *(Mis)Representing Islam: The racism and rhetoric of the broadsheet press*. Amsterdam: John Benjamins

Richardson, J.E. (2006) *Analysing Newspapers: An approach from critical discourse analysis*. Basingstoke: Palgrave Macmillan

Ritzer, G. (1998) *The McDonaldization Thesis*. London: Sage

Robertson, R. (1995) 'Glocalization: Time-space and homogeneity-heterogeneity', in M. Featherstone, S. Lash and R. Robertson (eds) *Global Modernities*. London: Sage, pp. 25–44

Rojek, C. (2001) *Celebrity*. London: Reaktion

Rooney, D. (2000) 'Thirty Years of Competition in the British Tabloid Press: The *Mirror* and the *Sun* 1968–98', in C. Sparks and J. Tulloch (eds) *Tabloid Tales: Global debates over media standards*. Oxford: Rowman and Littlefield, pp. 91–110

Rosenberry, J. and St. John II, B. (eds) (2010) *Public Journalism 2.0: The promise and reality of a citizen-engaged press*. Abingdon: Routledge

Ross, K. (2001) 'Women at Work: Journalism as en-gendered practice'. *Journalism Studies*, 2 (4): 531–44

Ross, K. (2005) 'Women in the Boyzone: Gender, news and herstory' in S. Allan (ed.) *Journalism: Critical issues*. Milton Keynes: Open University Press

Royal Commission on the Press (1949) *Report 1947–49*. Cmnd 7700. London: HMSO

Royal Commission on the Press (1962) *Report 1961–62*. Cmnd 1811. London: HMSO

Royal Commission on the Press (1977) *Report 1974–77*. Cmnd 6810. London: HMSO

Rozenberg (2004) *Privacy and the Press*. Oxford: Oxford University Press

Rubery, M. (ed.) (2009) *The Novelty of Newspapers: Victorian fiction after the invention of the news*. Oxford: Oxford University Press

Rudin, R. (2011) *Broadcasting in the 21st Century*. Basingstoke: Palgrave Macmillan

Runnymede Trust (2008) 'A Tale of Two Englands: "Race" and violent crime in the press'. London: Runnymede Trust. April. Available at http://www.runnymedetrust.org/ … /race-and-violent-crime-in-the-press.htm (accessed 14 July 2009)

Rusbridger, A. (2005) 'What are Newspapers For?' Hugo Young Lecture, University of Sheffield, 9 March. Available at http://image.guardian.co.uk/sys-files/Guardian/documents/2005/03/15/lecturesspeech.pdf (accessed 14 July 2009)

Ryle, J. (1997) 'Lost Explorers in the Disaster Zone'. *Guardian*, 22 November

Salter, L. (2005) 'The Communicative Structures of Journalism and Public Relations'. *Journalism: Theory, Practice and Criticism*, 6 (1): 90–106

Scannell, P. (1996) *Radio, Television and Modern Life: A phenomenological approach*. Oxford: Blackwell

Scannell, P. and Cardiff, D. (1991) *A Social History of Broadcasting, 1922–1939: Serving the nation*, vol. 1. Oxford: Blackwell

Schlesinger, P. (1978) *Putting Reality Together*. London: Constable

Schlesinger, P. (1990) 'Rethinking the Sociology of Journalism: Source strategies and the limits of media-centrism', in M. Ferguson (ed.) *Public Communication: The new imperatives*. London: Sage, pp. 61–83

Schlesinger, P. and Tumber, H. (1995) *Reporting Crime*. Oxford: Oxford University Press

Schlesinger, P., Murdock, G. and Elliott, P. (1983) *Televising Terrorism*. London: Comedia

Schudson, M. (1978) *Discovering the News: A social history of American Newspapers*. New York: Harper

Schudson, M. (2008) 'Public Spheres, Imagined Communities, and the Underdeveloped Historical Understanding of Journalism', in B. Zelizer (ed.) *Explorations in Communication and History*. Abingdon: Routledge, pp. 181–9

Searle, C. (1989) *Your Daily Dose: Racism in the* Sun. London: Campaign for Press and Broadcasting Freedom

Sebba, A. (1994) *Battling for the News: The rise of the woman reporter*. London: Sceptre

Seib, P. (2002). *The Global Journalist: News and conscience in a world of conflict*. Lanham, MD: Rowman and Littlefield

Seymour-Ure, C. (1974) *The Political Impact of the Mass Media*. London: Constable

Seymour-Ure, C. (2000) 'Northcliffe's Legacy', in P. Caterall, C. Semour-Ure and A. Smith (eds) *Northcliffe's Legacy*. Basingstoke: Macmillan, pp. 9–25

Shevelow, K. (1989) *Women and Print Culture*. London: Routledge

Siapera, E. (2011) *Understanding New Media*. London: Sage

Siebert, F.S. (1965) *Freedom of the Press in England 1476–1776: The rise and fall of government control*. Urbana, IL: Urbana University Press

Simpson, J. (2002) *News from No Man's Land: Reporting the world*. Basingstoke: Macmillan

Singer, J. (2009) 'Quality control'. *Journalism Practice*, 4 (2): 127–42

Singer, J.B., Hermida, A., Domingo, D., Heinonen, A., Paulussen, S., Quandt, T., Reich, Z. and Vujnovic, M. (2011) *Participatory Journalism: Guarding open gates at online newspapers*. New York: Wiley-Blackwell

Sloan, W.D. and Williams, J.H. (1994) *The Early American Press, 1690–1783*. Westport, CN: Greenwood Press

Smith, A. (1973) *The Shadow in the Cave*. London. Allen and Unwin

Smith, A. (1975) *Paper Voices: The popular press and social change, 1935–1965*. London: Chatto and Windus

Smith, A. (1979) *The Newspaper: An international history*. London: Thames & Hudson

Smith, A.(1980) *The Geopolitics of Information: How western culture dominates the world*. Oxford: Oxford University Press

Snoddy, R. (1993) *The Good, The Bad and The Unacceptable*. London: Faber and Faber

Snow, J. (1997) 'Is TV News Telling the Whole Story?' *Guardian*. Media Supplement, 27 January, p. 3

Society of Editors (2004) *Diversity in the Newsroom*. London: Society of Editors. Available at http://www.societyofeditors.co.uk/userfiles/file/Diversity%20in the%20Newsroom%20Report%20PDF.pdf (accessed 14 July 2009)

Sparks, C. (1998) 'Introduction: Tabloidization and the media'. *Javnost: The Public* 5 (3): 5–10

Sparks, C. (2000) 'Introduction: The panic over tabloid news', in C. Sparks and J. Tulloch (eds) *Tabloid Tales: Global debates over media standards*. Oxford: Rowman and Littlefield, pp. 1–40

Sparks, C. (2008) *Globalization, Development and the Mass Media*. London: Sage.

Sparks, C. and Tulloch, J. (2000) *Tabloid Tales: Global debates over media standards*. Oxford. Rowman and Littlefield

Sparrow, A. (2003) *Obscure Scribblers: A history of parliamentary journalism*. London: Politico's Publishing

Sreberny-Mohammadi, A. (1984) 'The World of News'. *Journal of Communication* (Winter): 121–34

Sreberny-Mohammadi, A., Stevenson, R. and Nordenstreng, K. (1984) 'The World of the News Study'. *Journal of Communication*, 34 (1): 120–42

Sreberny-Mohammadi, A., Wisbeck, D., McKenna, J. and Boyd-Barrett, O. (eds) (1997) *Media in a Global Context*. London: Hodder Education

Startt, J. (1991) *Journalists for Empire*. Westport, CT: Greenwood

Steen, R. (2007) *Sports Journalism: A multimedia primer*. Abingdon: Routledge

Stephenson, H. and Bromley, M. (eds) (1998) *Sex, Lies and Democracy: The press and the public*. Harlow: Longman

Stevenson, N., Jackson, P. and Brooks, K. (2001) *Understanding Men's Magazines*. Cambridge: Polity

Street, S. (2002) *A Concise History of British Radio*. Tiverton: Kelly

Sutton Trust (2006) 'The Educational Background of Leading Journalists'. Available at http://www.suttontrust.com/reports/Journalists-backgrounds-final-report.pdf (accesssed 14 July 2009)

Swithinbank, T. (2001) *Coming up from the streets: The story of* The Big Issue. London: Earthscan

Symon, J.D. (1914) *The Press and Its Story*. London: Seeley, Service and Co

Tae Kim, S. and Weaver, D. (2003) 'Reporting Globalization: A comparative analysis of sourcing patterns in five countries' newspapers'. *Gazette: The International Journal of Communication Studies*, 65 (2): 121–44

Taylor, P. (1999) *British Propaganda in the Twentieth Century*. Edinburgh: Edinburgh University Press

Taylor, S.J. (1992) *Shock, Horror: The tabloids in action*. London: Black Swan

Thomas, J. (2005) *Popular Newspapers, The Labour Party and British politics*. Abingdon: Routledge

Thussu, D.K. (2008) *News as Entertainment*. London: Sage

Thussu, D.K. and Freedman, D. (eds) (2003) *War and the Media: Reporting conflict 24/7*. London: Sage

Tomaselli, K. (2002) 'Journalism Education: Bridging media and cultural studies'. *Communication*, 28 (1): 22–8

Tomlinson, J. (1991) *Cultural Imperialism*. London: Pinter Publishers

Traber, M. and Nordensteng, K. (1992) *Few Voices, One World*. London: World

Tracey, M. (1977) *The Production of Political Television*. London: Routledge and Kegan Paul

Tucher, A. (2011) 'Teaching Journalism History to Journalists'. *Journalism Practice*, 5 (5): 551–65

Tuchman, G. (1973) 'Making news by doing work'. *American Journal of Sociology*, 79 (1): 110–31

Tuchman, G. (1978) *Making News: A study in the construction of reality*. New York: Free Press

Tumber, H. (1982) *Television and Riots*. London. Broadcasting Research Unit

Tumber, H. and Palmer, J. (2004) *Media at War: The Iraq crisis*. London: Sage

Tunstall, J. (1970) *The Westminster Lobby Correspondents*. London: Routledge and Kegan Paul

Tunstall, J. (1971) *Journalists at Work*. London: Constable

Tunstall, J. (1977) *The Media are America: Anglo-American media in the world*. London: Constable

Tunstall, J. (1996) *Newspaper Power: The new national press in Britain*. Oxford: Oxford University Press

Tunstall, J. (2008) *The Media were American: US mass media in decline*. Oxford: Oxford University Press

Tunstall, J. and Machin, D. (1999) *The Anglo-American Media Connection*. Oxford: Oxford University Press

Turner, G. (1990) *British Cultural Studies: An introduction*. London: Routledge

Turner, G. (2004) *Understanding Celebrity*. London: Sage

Ursell, G.D.M. (2001) 'Dumbing Down or Shaping Up? New technologies, new media, new journalism'. *Journalism: Theory, Practice and Criticism* 2 (2): 174–96

Ursell, G.D.M. (2003) 'Creating Value and Valuing Creation in Contemporary UK Television: Or "dumbing down" the workforce'. *Journalism Studies*, 4 (1): 31–46

Voltmer, K. (2011) *The Media in Transitional Democracies*. Cambridge: Polity

Wahl-Jorgensen, K. and Hanitszch, T. (2009) *Handbook of Journalism Studies*. London: Routledge

Ward, S. J. and Wasserman, H. (eds.) (2010) *Media Ethics Beyond Borders: A global perspective*. Abingdon: Routledge

Waugh, E. (1938) *Scoop*. London: Chapman and Hall

Weaver, D.H. (ed.) (1998) *The Global Journalist: News people around the world*. Cresskill, NJ: Hampton Press

Weaver, D.H. and Willnat, L. (eds) (2012) *The Global Journalist in the 21st Century*. London: Routledge

Whale, J. (1969) *The Eye Half Shut*. Basingstoke: Macmillan

White, C.L. (1970) *Women's Magazines 1693–1968*. London: Michael Joseph

Wiener, J. (ed.) (1988) *Papers for the Millions: The new journalism in Britain, 1850–1914*. New York: Greenwood

Wiener, J. and Hampton, M. (eds) (2007) *Anglo-American Media Interactions 1850–1900*. Basingstoke: Palgrave Macmillan

Williams, A., Wardle, C. and Wahl-Jorgenssen, K. (2011) 'The Limits of Audience Participation: UGC@the BBC', in B. Franklin and M. Carlson

Journalists, Sources and Credibility: New perspectives. Abingdon: Routledge, pp. 152–66

Williams, F. (1957) *Dangerous Estate.* Harlow: Longman Green

Williams, K. (1999) 'Teaching Journalism in Britain', in G. Philo (ed.) *Message Received: Glasgow Media Group, research 1993–98.* Harlow: Longman

Williams, R. (1958) *Culture and Society 1780–1950.* London: Chatto and Windus

Williams, R. (1961) *The Long Revolution.* Harmondsworth: Penguin

Williams, R. (1974) *Television: Technology and cultural form.* London: Fontana

Wilson, J. (1996) *Understanding Journalism: A guide to issues.* London: Routledge

Winston, B. (1998) *Media, Technology and Society.* London: Routledge

Winston, B. (2002) 'Towards Tabloidization: Glasgow revisited, 1975–2001'. *Journalism Studies* 3 (1): 5–20

Wintour, C. (1989) *The Rise and Fall of Fleet Street.* London: Hutchinson

Witschge, T. Phillips, A. and Lee-Wright, P. (eds) (2011) *Changing Journalism.* Abingdon: Routledge

Worcester, R.M. (1998) 'Demographics and Values: What the British public reads and what it thinks about its newspapers', in H. Stephenson and M. Bromley (eds) *Sex, Lies and Democracy: The press and the public.* Harlow: Longman, pp. 39–48.

Wu, H.D. (2004) 'The World's Windows to the World: An overview of 44 nations' international news coverage', in C. Patterson and A. Sreberny (eds) *International News in the Twenty First Century.* Luton: University of Luton Press, pp. 95–110

Wyndham Goldie, G. (1977) *Facing the Nation: Television and Politics 1936–1976.* London: Bodley Head

Zelizer, B. (2004) *Taking Journalism Seriously: News and the academy.* London: Sage

Zelizer, B. and Allan, S. (eds) (2002) *Journalism After September 11.* London: Routledge

Zhu, J., Weaver, D.H., Lo, V., Chen, C. and Wu, W. (1997) 'Individual, Organizational and Societal Influences on Media Role Perceptions: A comparative study of journalists in China, Taiwan and the United States'. *Journalism and Mass Communication Quarterly* 74: 84–96

van Zoonen, L. (1994) *Feminist Media Studies.* London: Sage

van Zoonen, L. (1998) ' "One of the Girls": The changing gender of journalism', in C. Carter, G. Branson and S. Allan (eds) *News, Gender and Power.* London: Routledge, pp. 33–46

INDEX